ASTOUNDING NEW DISCOVERIES

Mathematics Proves
Holy Scriptures

by
KARL SABIERS, M.A.

New England Bible Sales
262 Quaker Road
Sidney ME 04330
NewEnglandBibleSales.com
jptbooks@gmail.com

Foreword

Some discoveries are interesting, some
have a practical use, and some have
powerful potential. Ivan Panin's
discovery has all three.

Two languages in the world have a
numeric value for every letter -- Hebrew
and Greek. These have been used for
centuries in business transactions

Ivan Panin found complex mathematical
patterns throughout the Greek text of the
Bible.

Assuming that the Greek manuscripts
whose text fit the complex mathematical
patterns would be the accurate copies,
Ivan Panin produced a Greek text. This
was then translated into English in 1914.

The similarity between the English
Standard Version Bible that used the
latest in textual scholarship and Panin's
that used the numerical "watermark" is
amazing. Comparing Panin's NT with
the Newberry Bible shows much
sameness.

Some information Karl Sabiers states
about the human body may need to be
updated; some statements are his opinion;
on the whole very interesting reading.

Jim Thompson 2012

CONTENTS

Astounding New Discoveries

CHAPTER ONE

The Matter Stated

The newly discovered facts which form the basis for the subject matter of this book are supremely important and highly significant. They are facts which scientifically prove that the Bible could not possibly have been written by mere human beings alone, but that it is a supernatural, God inspired, God given book! They are facts which enable us to see before our very eyes an actual scientific demonstration of the divine, verbal inspiration of the Bible. The discoveries of facts so important as these are indeed "Astounding New Discoveries."

The newly revealed facts are facts which have been discovered beneath the very surface of the original Bible text. They are facts which have been mysteriously and peculiarly hidden for hundreds of years. They are facts which have been revealed by the hundreds and thousands, not merely by the twos or threes or half dozens. They are facts which are baffling and confounding atheists and agnostics—facts which no living person has been able to discredit or refute. They are facts which are causing skeptical and modernistic thinkers to accept the Bible as a supernatural, God inspired book. They are facts which, without a doubt, constitute some of the greatest discoveries of all time. Is it any wonder that the discoveries of facts such as these are called "Astounding New Discoveries?"

The foregoing statements in regard to the profound newly discovered facts no doubt cause the majority of readers to ask numerous questions.

—What are the amazing facts which have been discovered beneath the very surface of the original Bible text?

—How do these facts scientifically prove that the Bible could not possibly have been written by mere human beings alone, but that it is a supernatural, God inspired book?

—Who discovered the facts?
—How and when were they discovered?
—Why were they not discovered until recently?
—How do they affect us?

These and various other questions no doubt arise in the minds of those who are somewhat curious about the amazing newly discovered facts. However, before one learns what these facts are—before an attempt is made to answer any or all of these questions, it is necessary to remind or inform the reader of—

THE GREAT BIBLE "CLAIM" CONCERNING ITSELF

There can be no doubt that the Bible "claims" to be a supernatural, God inspired, God given book. The Bible declares that "All scripture is given by inspiration of God." II Timothy 3:16. The expression, "given by inspiration of God" is the translation of one Greek word "theopneustos," which means literally "God-breathed." The great Bible claim then, is that "all scripture," the entire Bible, "is God-breathed."

The Bible claims that the writers of Scripture, wrote, not of their own will, but only as they were "moved" or "controlled" by the Holy Spirit of God. II Peter 1:21 declares that the Scripture came "not . . . by the will of man, but holy men of God spake as they were moved by the Holy Spirit." Another translation of this same passage declares that no Scripture "was ever borne by man's will; but men spake from God, being borne on by the Holy Spirit."

The Bible claims that the words which the prophets wrote were not their own words but that they were the very words of God Himself. The Person speaking was God, not man. God was speaking merely **"by"** or **"through"** man. "God . . . spake in time past unto the fathers by the prophets." Hebrews 1:1. "He (the Lord God) spake by the mouth of His holy prophets." Luke 1:70. "The Spirit of the Lord spake by me, and His word (not the writer's own word) was in my tongue." II Samuel 23:1, 2. "Behold I (God) have put my words in thy mouth." Jeremiah 1:9. "Thou shalt speak my words (God's words) unto them." Ezekiel 2:7. A death penalty was pronounced upon the prophet who should add any of his own words to God's words. God declared, "the prophet, which shall presume to speak a word in my name, which I have not commanded him to speak, . . . even that prophet shall die." Deuteronomy 18:20. God said to Moses, "Ye shall not add unto the word which I command you, neither shall ye diminish ought from it." Deuteronomy 4:2. Thus the Bible clearly distinguishes itself from the word of men. It claims that its words are the very words of God Himself and that men were merely the instru-ments or mouthpieces "by" or "through" which God "breathed" His Word. The prophets merely recorded the words they received from God. They did not always understand the full significance of what they wrote, for they "diligently" "searched" their own writings so that they might understand more perfectly. I Peter 1:10-12.

The Apostle Paul declares, "the things that I write unto you are the commandments of the Lord"—not his own commandments. I Corinthians 14:37. "We speak, not in the words which man's wisdom teacheth, but which the Holy Ghost teacheth." I Cor-inthians 2:13. "Ye heard of us . . . not the word of men, but . . . the word of God." I Thessalonians 2:13. The phrase, "Word of God" occurs frequently and is always especially significant. Statements such as "Thus saith the Lord," "God said," and similar expressions, occur more than 2,500 times in the entire Bible. The Scripture is to be received "not as the word of men, but as it is in truth, the word of God." Thus, the Bible makes startling claims for itself—it actually claims to be a supernatural, God breathed, God given book—the very Word of God Himself. This is the unmistakable language of the Bible. Numerous other Biblical statements could be given in support of this claim. However, those already presented are sufficient for the present purpose.

There can be no doubt about what the Bible "claims" concerning itself. However, many have raised the question—"Is that claim actually true?" Is the Bible actually the very Word of God?"

The facts which have been recently discovered beneath the very surface of the original Bible text now scientifically prove and demonstrate before our very eyes that the Bible claim is true—that the Bible actually is a supernatural, God inspired book!

Various questions concerning the newly discovered facts were mentioned in a preceding paragraph. The first of these questions can now be discussed and answered.

CHAPTER TWO

What Are The Newly Discovered Facts?

What are the amazing facts which have been discovered beneath the very surface of the original Bible text? What are these facts which scientifically prove that the Bible could not possibly have been written by mere human beings alone, but that it is a supernatural, God inspired, God given book?

It has been stated that the facts have been mysteriously hidden beneath the very surface of the original Bible text. In order to understand what these facts are, it will be necessary to know—

THE MEANING OF THE TERM "ORIGINAL BIBLE TEXT"

Most persons are acquainted with the fact that the Bible contains two main divisions — the Old Testament, and the New Testament. Strange as it may seem, these two main divisions of the Bible were originally written in different languages. The Old Testament was originally written in Hebrew while the New Testament was written in Greek. By the term "original Bible text" is meant the Hebrew and

Greek text of the Bible—the words of the writers in the original languages, not their words translated into some other language. The facts, then, have been discovered beneath the surface of the **Hebrew** Old Testament text and the **Greek** New Testament text of the Bible.

Before the reader can understand what the facts are (the facts which have been mysteriously concealed in the Hebrew and Greek Bible text) it is necessary to carefully observe—

A PECULIAR CHARACTERISTIC OF THE HEBREW AND GREEK LANGUAGES

Many of the newly discovered facts have a direct bearing on the unusual characteristic of these languages. The following comparison is made with the English in order that the peculiarity of the Hebrew and Greek might be clearly understood.

In English there are twenty-six letters in the alphabet, a, b, c, d, e, f, g, h, etc. In addition to these twenty-six letters we use the numbers 1, 2, 3, 4, 5, 6, 7, 8, 9, 0. These figures are the Arabic symbols used for the purpose of expressing "numbers."

The Hebrew and Greek languages do not have a system like this. These languages have only the letters of their alphabets, but do not have additional symbols or figures such as 1, 2, 3, 4, etc. which express numbers. Instead of using special figures, the Hebrew and Greek languages use the letters of their alphabets to express or represent numbers. Thus the letters of their alphabets serve a twofold purpose—they are used to represent or express numbers as well as to write words. Every letter of the Hebrew and Greek alphabets represents a certain "number." In other words, each letter is assigned a "numeric value." This is the peculiar characteristic of these languages.

The Hebrew alphabet has 22 letters and the Greek alphabet 24.

Below are listed the 22 letters of the Hebrew alphabet. Beside each letter is its "numeric value"— the "number" which it represents.

א 1	ל 30		
ב 2	מ * .... ם * 40		
ג 3	נ * .... ן * 50		
ד 4	ס 60		
ה 5	ע 70		
ו 6	פ * .... ף * 80		
ז 7	צ * .... ץ * 90		
ח 8	ק 100		
ט 9	ר 200		
י 10	ש 300		
כ * .... ך * 20	ת 400		

(*When the following letters כ מ נ פ צ 20, 40, 50, 80, 90, are used at the end of words they are written in slightly different, abbreviated forms, as follows: ך ם ן ף ץ)

Below are listed the 24 letters of the Greek alphabet. Beside each letter is its "numeric value"—the
"number" which it represents.

A α	 1	N ν	 50
B β	 2	Ξ ξ	 60
Γ γ	 3	O o	 70
Δ δ	 4	Π π	 80
E ε	 5	P ϱ	 100
Z ζ	 7	Σ σ * ___ ς *	 200
H η	 8	T τ	 300
Θ ϑ	 9	Y υ	 400
I ι	 10	Φ φ	 500
K κ	 20	X χ	 600
Λ λ	 30	Ψ ψ	 700
M μ	 40	Ω ω	 800

(*When the Greek letter σ is used at the
end of a word it is written in a different
form — ς)

The Hebrew and Greek letters then, in addition
to expressing sounds, also express the numbers 1, 2, 3,
4, 5, etc. Each letter represents a certain "number"—
it has a definite "numeric value." For example, in
Greek the number one hundred forty-four is written
ϱ μ δ for these letters have the following numeric
values   ϱ - 100   μ - 40   δ - 4

The reader can easily understand that since each
Greek and Hebrew letter has a numeric value, each
word likewise has a numeric value, for each word of

course is made up of one or more letters. For example, the Greek word 'Ιησοῦς which means "Jesus" has a numeric value of 888. Why? Because the numeric values of the six Greek letters in the word 'Ιησοῦς Jesus, when added, total 888.

'Ι	η	σ	ο	ῦ	ς	Total
10	8	200	70	400	200	888

Thus the numeric value of this Greek word 'Ιησοῦς Jesus, is 888. In connection with this it is interesting to note that Satan's number or the number of the anti-Christ is 666—a strange comparison indeed. Revelation 13:18

Every Greek and Hebrew word, then, in addition to expressing some idea, also has a numeric value which is obtained by adding the numeric values of the special letters in each particular word.

The reader can easily understand that since every word in the Hebrew and Greek has a numeric value, as shown in the above example, each sentence likewise has a definite arithmetical sum or numeric value, for each sentence of course is composed of a number of words. The numeric value of a sentence is obtained by adding the numeric value of each word contained therein. The following Greek sentence, "Εδάκρυσεν ὁ 'Ιησοῦς" is given as an example.

If this were translated word for word into English it would read, "Wept the Jesus." In the King James or Authorized Version of the Bible, it is translated "Jesus wept." John 11:35.

Ἐδάκρυσεν ὁ Ἰησοῦς   Total
785   70   888   1743

The total of the numeric values of the three words is 1743. Thus the numeric value of the sentence is 1743.

Just as each sentence has a numeric value, so each paragraph and each passage has a numeric value. In precisely the same way, each of the sixty-six books of the Bible has a numeric value.

Thus the peculiar characteristic of both the Hebrew and Greek languages is that the letters, words, sentences, paragraphs, passages, etc., have "numeric values."

Now there is one number in particular to which the reader's attention is called. It is a number which occurs in Scripture more times than any other. It is the number "seven." From the first book of the Bible through the last book, "seven" is by far the outstanding number. For example, the Sabbath was the seventh day. In Egypt there were seven years of plenty and seven years of famine. When the city of Jericho was captured, the people and seven priests who had seven trumpets marched around the city seven times. Every seventh year the land of the Israelites was not to be cultivated or planted. Solomon was seven years building the temple. After its completion he held the feast for seven days. Naaman washed seven times in the river.

In the book of Revelation, the last book of the Bible, this number is especially outstanding. **Seven**

churches, seven lampstands, seven seals, seven trumpets, seven vials, seven stars, seven spirits, etc., are
mentioned. In all, the number seven occurs in the
book of Revelation more than fifty times.

It has long been known that the number seven
occurs in the Bible in this particular manner more
frequently than any other number. However, only
recently it has been discovered that this same number
also occurs in a mysterious and peculiar manner beneath the very surface of the Hebrew Old Testament
text and the Greek New Testament text of the Bible.

When it is stated that the sevens occur in a
peculiar manner "beneath the surface" of the original
Bible text, we mean that they occur in such a way
that they are not noticed or discovered by merely
"reading" the surface, or words. The sevens are
strangely out of the sight of ordinary Hebrew and
Greek readers. They are mysteriously hidden. Thousands
who have read and studied the original Hebrew and
Greek text of the Bible have passed by these strange
occurrences of the number seven without even noticing or knowing of their presence. These sevens are
so deeply concealed that special searching and investigation and special counting are necessary in order to
find them. Thus they are said to occur "beneath the
surface" or "in the structure" of the text because they
are beyond the observation and view of ordinary
Hebrew and Greek readers.

It has been discovered that thousands of these
sevens are mysteriously hidden in the structure of the
text. Some of the sevens are strangely concealed in

the unusual system of numbers—in the "numeric values" of the Hebrew and Greek letters, words, sentences, paragraphs and passages of the text, while other sevens are hidden in other remarkable and peculiar ways.

These sevens beneath the surface of the original Hebrew and Greek Bible text are the amazing newly discovered facts. The astounding new discoveries are numerical discoveries—discoveries having to do with numbers. The recently revealed numerical facts or sevens, in a most extraordinary way, enable us to see before our very eyes an actual scientific demonstration of the divine verbal inspiration of the Bible.

The reader is given examples of these newly discovered numerical facts before he learns how they scientifically prove that the Bible is a supernatural, God breathed book.

CHAPTER THREE

Examples Of Facts Discovered Beneath The Surface Of The First Verse In The Old Testament And The First Chapters In The New Testament

The following are examples of the newly dis-covered facts or "sevens" which occur in a peculiar manner beneath the surface of the **Hebrew text** of the first verse in the Old Testament—the very first verse in the Bible.

BOOK OF GENESIS, CHAPTER ONE, VERSE 1

"In the beginning God created the heavens and the earth."

The first "sevens" pointed out occur in a strange manner in the "numeric values" of various words and letters of the verse. It has already been stated and explained that each Hebrew and Greek word has a "numeric value." The Greek word Ἰησοῦς Jesus, was given as an example, and its numeric value was seen to be 888.

Below are the Hebrew words of the very first verse in the Bible. The words are taken from their line position and placed in a column so that the "numeric value" of each word may be more easily shown.

	Numeric Value	
בראשית	913	In the beginning
ברא	203	Created
אלהים	86	God
את	401	(An indefinite article which is not translatable)
השמים	395	The heavens
ואת	407	And (with indefinite article)
הארץ	296	The earth.

(The Hebrew reads from right to left instead of left to right as we are accustomed to reading. Thus the first letter of each Hebrew word is on the right, not on the left.)

There are three important nouns in this first verse —'God', 'heaven' and 'earth.' The numeric values of these three nouns are 86, 395, 296, respectively. When these three numeric values are added, the total value is found to be a number which divides perfectly by 7—a number which is a multiple of 7. The total numeric value of the three words, strange as it may seem, is exactly 777, which of course is 111 7's.

Is it not strange that the numeric value of these words is a value which divides perfectly by seven— a value which is an exact multiple of seven? Notice that the numeric value of the words is not 776 or 778, but exactly 777. If the numeric value were 776 or 778 it would not divide evenly by 7.

Here the number seven occurs in a strange manner beneath the surface, beyond the view of those
who merely "read" the words or surface of the Hebrew
text. It is mysteriously hidden in the numeric value
of the three words and is passed by unnoticed unless
it is discovered by special investigation and special
counting.

Each numerical "fact" or "seven" discovered in
the structure of the text is called a "feature"—a
"numeric feature." This, then, is feature one. It is
repeated below to place it in a list with other numeric
features which have been discovered beneath the
surface of the first verse in the Old Testament.

FEATURE ONE

The numeric value of the
three important Hebrew
nouns, "God," "heaven,"
"earth," is exactly ....777 or   111   7's

FEATURE TWO

It is strange to note that the
numeric value of the verb in
the first verse of Genesis is
also a number which divides
perfectly by 7—a number
which is an exact multiple
of 7. The numeric value of
the Hebrew verb "created"
is exactly ....203 or   29   7's

FEATURE THREE

Strange to say, the numeric value of the first, middle, and last Hebrew letters in this first verse is also a number which divides evenly by 7. The numeric value of these three letters is exactly 133   or   19   7's

FEATURE FOUR

The numeric value of the first and last letters of all of the seven words in this verse is also a number which divides perfectly by 7. Their numeric value is exactly 1,393   or   199   7's
Notice the numeric value is not 1,392 or 1,394 but 1,393, always a number which is an exact multiple of 7.

FEATURE FIVE

The number 1,393 which is the numeric value of the first and last letters of all the seven words, divides in the following manner. The numeric value of the first and last letters of the first word and the last word is a number which divides evenly by 7. Their numeric value is exactly 497   or   71   7's

The numeric value of the first and last letters of the words remaining between the first and last words also divides perfectly by 7. Their numeric value is 896   or   128   7's (497 plus 896 equals 1,393)

FEATURE SIX

The Hebrew participle "ETH" which is not translatable into English, occurs twice in the sentence of seven words. The article "the" also occurs twice. The numeric value of these two words which occur twice also divides by 7. Their numeric value is exactly 406   or   58   7's

FEATURE SEVEN

The last letters of the first and last words have a numeric value of exactly 490   or   70   7's

These numeric facts or sevens are indeed beyond the view of mere "readers" of the Hebrew text. They are truly mysteriously hidden beneath the surface and can be discovered only by special searching and calculations.

The above features were discovered in the "numeric values" of the Hebrew letters and words. However, the number seven is also concealed in various other ways in the structure of this first Bible verse. Examples are given below.

FEATURE EIGHT

It is indeed strange to note
that the number of Hebrew
words in this verse is not 6,
not 8, but exactly 7

FEATURE NINE

The total number of Hebrew
letters in these seven words
also divides perfectly by
seven—is an exact multiple
of 7. The number of letters
is exactly 28   or   4   7's

FEATURE TEN

The first three of these seven
Hebrew words contain the
the subject and predicate of
the sentence.   These three
words are translated — "In
the beginning God created."
The number of **letters** in
these   first   three   Hebrew
words is exactly 14   or   2   7's
The last four of these seven
words contain the object of
the sentence.   These four
words are translated "the—
heavens and the earth." The
number of **letters** in these
last four Hebrew words is..............14   or   2   7's

FEATURE ELEVEN

These last four Hebrew words consist of two objects. The first is "the heavens," and the second is "and the earth." The number of letters in the first object is exactly ....7 The number of letters in the second object in the Hebrew is --7

FEATURE TWELVE

The three leading words in this verse of seven words are "God" — the subject — and "heavens" and "earth" — the objects. The number of letters in these three Hebrew words is exactly 14   or   2   7's The number of letters in the other four words of the verse is ---------------------------------14   or   2   7's

FEATURE THIRTEEN

The shortest word is in the middle. The number of letters in this word and the word to its left is exactly 7

FEATURE FOURTEEN

The number of letters in the middle word and the word to its right is exactly ....____7

These sevens—these numeric features or facts—are indeed strangely hidden "beneath the surface." They are truly beyond the view of ordinary readers of the Hebrew text and are discovered only by special investigation and counting.

The above are only a few examples of the many amazing numeric facts which have been discovered in the structure of this first verse of only seven Hebrew words. Literally dozens of other phenomenal numeric features strangely underlie the structure of this verse.

Examples of these newly discovered facts or numerical features should be pointed out from other passages before the reader learns how they **scientifically** prove that the Bible could not possibly have been written by mere human beings alone, but that it is a supernatural, God inspired, God given book.

The following are examples of the newly discovered facts or "sevens" which occur in a peculiar manner beneath the surface of the **Greek** text of the first verses in the New Testament.

BOOK OF MATTHEW, CHAPTER ONE, VERSES 1-17

The Account of Christ's Genealogy

The first seventeen verses in the book of Matthew form a natural, logical division by themselves, for they deal with one particular subject, namely, the genealogy of Christ. There are seventy-two Greek **vocabulary** words in these first seventeen verses. The first fact or "seven" pointed out is strangely hidden in the total "numeric value" of these seventy-two Greek vocabulary words.

It must be remembered that the number of vocabulary words in a passage is usually different from the **total number of words** in a passage. The vocabulary words are the different words used. For instance, the word "and" is one word in the vocabulary, but it may be repeated many times in the passage itself. A man may have a vocabulary of only five hundred words. With these five hundred different words he may write an essay of four thousand words. Some of the words, such as "and," "for," "by," etc., may be used over and over again. The number of vocabulary words, or the number of different words used in a passage, is thus not the same as the total number of words used.

It has already been stated that there are seventy-two Greek vocabulary words in these first seventeen verses of Matthew, and the first fact or "seven" is strangely concealed in the "numeric value" of these words.

FEATURE ONE

It is amazing to note that the total numeric value of these 72 words is also a number which divides perfectly by 7—a number which is an exact multiple of 7. The numeric value of these words is exactly 42,364   or   6,052   7's

Notice the number is not 42,363, or 42,365, but exactly 42,364. Neither of the first two numbers divides evenly by 7. If even **one** Greek letter were taken out or exchanged for another letter, the numeric value would be changed.

FEATURE TWO

The 72 Greek vocabulary words in the first seventeen verses of Matthew occur in 90 forms. (Greek words are written in various forms to give slightly different meanings. For example, the word 'Ιησοῦς Jesus, is sometimes written 'Ιησοῦ which means "of Jesus." This then is a different form of the word "Jesus.") The 72 vocabulary words mentioned above occur in 90 forms. It is astonishing to note that the **numeric value** of the 90 forms is also a number which is a multiple of 7. The numeric value of these forms is exactly ....54,075 or 7,725 7's

These particular features of 7's occur beneath the surface of the passage in the "numeric values." The number 7 also underlies the text in many other remarkable ways.

FEATURE THREE
Of these 72 Greek vocabulary words in the first seventeen verses of Matthew the number of words which are nouns is exactly 56   or   8   7's

FEATURE FOUR
The Greek word "the" occurs most frequently in the passage. The number of times it occurs is exactly................56   or   8   7's

FEATURE FIVE
The number of different forms in which the article "the" occurs is exactly 7

These first seventeen verses of the Greek New Testament consist of two main sections. (I) Verses 1-11. (II)   Verses 12-17. Each section contains amazing numeric features in the structure of its text.

The following are a few examples of the facts or "sevens" which have been discovered beneath the surface of the first main section, verses 1-11.

FEATURE SIX
The number of Greek vocabulary words used in the first eleven verses is not 48, not 50, but exactly 49   or   7   7'

FEATURE SEVEN
Of these 49 words the number which begin with a
vowel is exactly ....28 or   4   7's
The number of words which
begin with a consonant is ....21 or   3   7's

FEATURE EIGHT
The number of letters in
these 49 words is exactly ....266 or   38   7's

FEATURE NINE   '
Of these 266 letters of the
vocabulary words, the num-
ber of vowels is exactly ....140 or   20   7's

Of these 266 letters of the
vocabulary, the number of
consonants is ....126 or   18   7's

FEATURE TEN
Of these 49 Greek vocab-
ulary words in the first eleven
verses, the number of words
which occur more than once
is exactly ....35 or   5   7's
The number of words which
occur only once is ....14 or   2   7's

FEATURE ELEVEN
Of these 49 Greek vocab-
ulary words the number
which appear in only one
form is exactly ....42 or   6   7's
The number which appear in
more than one form is 7

FEATURE TWELVE
Of the 49 Greek vocab-
ulary words, the number
which are nouns is exactly 42   or   6   7's
The number which are not
nouns is 7

FEATURE THIRTEEN
Of the 42 nouns in the first
eleven verses, the number
which are proper names is
exactly 35   or   5   7's
The number which are com-
mon nouns is 7

FEATURE FOURTEEN
The number of Greek letters
in these 7 common nouns is
exactly 49   or   7   7's
It is amazing to note that in
these 7 common nouns alone,
there   are   more   than   20
numeric features

FEATURE FIFTEEN
The number of times the 35
proper names (Feature Thir-
teen) occur is exactly 63   or   9   7's

FEATURE SIXTEEN
Of the 35 proper names in
the vocabulary of the first
eleven verses of Matthew,
the number of male names
is exactly 28   or   4   7's

The number which are not
male names is 7

FEATURE SEVENTEEN
The number of times these
28 male names occur is exactly........56   or   8   7's

FEATURE EIGHTEEN
In these first 11 verses, three
women are mentioned — Ta-
mar, Rahab, and Ruth. The
number of Greek letters in
these three names is exactly............14   or   2   7's

FEATURE NINETEEN
Just one city is named in
this passage, namely, Babylon
The number of Greek letters
in this word is exactly 7

It was stated that the first seventeen verses in the
Greek New Testament consist of two main sections.
(I) Verses 1-11. (II) Verses 12-17. The above are
merely a few examples of the many amazing numerical
features which have been discovered beneath the surface of this first section of eleven verses. The very
structure of the passage is literally saturated with
phenomenal occurrences of the number seven. The
second section, verses 12-17 contains equally profound
numeric features of its own. However, it is needless to
enumerate more examples from this particular passage.

Before it is shown how these facts or sevens
scientifically prove the divine inspiration of the Bible,
additional examples are given from the Greek text of
other New Testament passages.

The section following the first seventeen verses of Matthew is verses 18-25.

BOOK OF MATTHEW, CHAPTER ONE, VERSES 18-25

The Account of Christ's Birth

FEATURE ONE

The number of Greek words
in this passage is exactly 161   or   23   7's

FEATURE TWO

The numeric value of these
161 words is exactly ....93,394 or 13,342   7's

FEATURE THREE

The number of Greek vocabulary words in this passage
is exactly ....77 or   11   7's

FEATURE FOUR

The numeric value of the 77
vocabulary words is a number
which divides evenly by
seven. The numeric value
is exactly ....51,247 or 7,321   7's

FEATURE FIVE

The six Greek words found
in this passage, but found
nowhere else in the book of
Matthew have a numeric
value of exactly 5,005   or   715   7's

FEATURE SIX
The number of letters in these six Greek words is exactly ....56 or 8 7's

FEATURE SEVEN
The one word found nowhere else in the New Testament is the Greek word "Emmanuel." It has a numeric value of exactly ....644 or 92 7's

FEATURE EIGHT
The number of forms in which these 161 words of the passage occur is exactly ....105 or 15 7's

FEATURE NINE
The numeric value of the 105 forms is exactly ....65,429 or 9,347 7's

FEATURE TEN
Of the 105 forms, the number of verbs is exactly ....35 or 5 7's

FEATURE ELEVEN
Of the 105 forms, the number of proper names is exactly..........7

FEATURE TWELVE
The number of Greek letters in these 7 proper names is ....42 or 6 7's

FEATURE THIRTEEN
The number of forms found
in this passage, but found
nowhere else in Matthew is 14   or   2   7's

FEATURE FOURTEEN
The numeric value of these
14 forms is exactly 8,715   or   1,245   7's

FEATURE FIFTEEN
Of the 77 Greek vocabulary
words, the number of words
the angel used in speaking
to Joseph is exactly 28   or   4   7's

FEATURE SIXTEEN
The numeric value of all the
words the angel used is 21,042   or   3,006   7's

FEATURE SEVENTEEN
The number of forms the
angel used is exactly 35   or   5   7's

FEATURE EIGHTEEN
The number of Greek letters
in these 35 forms which are
used by the angel is exactly 168   or   24   7's

FEATURE NINETEEN
The numeric value of the 35
forms which are used by the
angel is exactly 19,397   or   2,771   7's

Even the angel's little speech has amazing numerical features all of its own. They are entirely separate
from the rest of the passage, yet they form a part of the
numerical features of the whole passage. They are
intertwined in such a way that the entire passage contains remarkable occurrences of the number seven.

The above nineteen features are merely a few
examples of the many phenomenal numeric facts which
have been discovered beneath the surface of this one
passage, Matthew, Chapter One, verses 18-25. The
number seven strangely underlies the very structure
of the text in every conceivable manner. The Greek
letters and words are literally permeated with amazing
occurrences of the number seven.

Following are examples of numerical facts which
are strangely hidden in the second chapter of Matthew.

BOOK OF MATTHEW, THE ENTIRE SECOND CHAPTER

The Account Of Christ's Childhood

FEATURE ONE
The number of Greek vocabulary words in the second
chapter of Matthew is exactly 161   or   23   7's

FEATURE TWO
The number of Greek letters
in these 161 words is exactly 896   or   128   7's

FEATURE THREE
The numeric value of the 161
vocabulary words is exactly ..123,529   or   17,647   7's

FEATURE FOUR
The number of forms in the
passage is exactly ....238 or   34   7's

FEATURE FIVE
The numeric value of the
forms is exactly ....166,985 or 23,855   7's

There are several paragraphs in the second chapter of Matthew, and each paragraph has amazing
numerical features all of its own. They are separate
from the rest of the passage, yet in a peculiar and intricate way, they form a part of the amazing features
of the whole chapter. They are intertwined in such
a phenomenal way that the entire chapter is one great
mathematical unit which consists of amazing numerical
facts.

For example, the number of
Greek vocabulary words in
the first six verses divides
perfectly by 7. The number
of vocabulary words is exactly.........56 or   8   7's

There are three speeches in the chapter. Herod
speaks, the wise men speak, the angel speaks. Each
speech shows numeric features in itself, yet each forms
only part of the chapter, which as a whole has phenomenal features of its own. Each division alone shows the
same numeric phenomena found in the chapter as a
whole.

These are certainly remarkable and startling occurrences of the number seven in the very structure of
the text. They are so deeply and peculiarly hidden

that the reader can well understand how thousands of
Greek and Hebrew readers could pass them by without
noticing them.

The preceding numerical features from the second
chapter of Matthew do not form a complete list by any
means. They are merely a few examples of the interesting features which permeate and underlie the
structure of this passage.

In the preceding pages of this book the reader
has been given a small conception of the thousands of
amazing facts which have been found in the very
structure of Bible passages.

THE EXTENT OF THESE NUMERICAL
FEATURES

It has been discovered that amazing numerical
facts occur beneath the surface of the original Bible
text from the very first verse in Genesis through the
very last verse in Revelation. Phenomenal mathematical features, similar to the examples already presented,
underlie and pervade the text of every one of the
sixty-six Bible books. They occur in the very structure
of every paragraph in the entire Bible, not in the
paragraphs only, but often in the many sub-divisions
of paragraphs. Often single verses are literally teem-
ing and saturated with astounding numerical facts.
These features extend to all parts of the text, vocabulary, grammatical forms, parts of speech, etc. Often
as many as a hundred or more numeric features are
strangely hidden beneath the surface of passages which
consist of no more than 175 words. Actually thousands of the numerical facts have been discovered—

they are so abundant that more than 40,000 pages have been required to contain the calculations used in discovering and enumerating the features of the New Testament, alone.

The examples in the preceding pages—examples from the first verse in Genesis and the first passages in the New Testament—have shown how the numerical facts or sevens underlie the structure of **single Bible passages.** However, this is only one particular manner in which the sevens occur. It has been discovered that they occur beneath the surface of the text in dozens of other ways.

The next chapter is devoted to one other particular manner in which the sevens are found in the structure of the Bible text. Then the reader will be prepared to learn the significance of these newly discovered facts—how they scientifically prove the Bible could not possibly have been written by mere human beings alone, but it is a supernatural, God inspired, God given book.

In the addenda there are additional abbreviated examples of the same type of numeric discoveries as are presented in this chapter—discoveries of facts which occur beneath the surface of **single Bible passages.** The examples in the addenda are facts discovered in the structure of passages from the Book of Mark, and are very interesting indeed. The reader may find it helpful if he refers to them before beginning the next chapter which discusses another manner in which the facts underlie the original Bible text.

CHAPTER FOUR

Another Manner In Which The Newly Discovered Facts Occur Beneath The Surface Of The Original Bible Text

The examples in the preceding two chapters are examples of numerical facts which occur beneath the surface of **single passages.** The following are examples of features which occur in a different manner. They are features which are not confined to single passages, but are features which occur in the structure of **special words**—words which are separated by great distances, appearing in many different books of the Bible.

EXAMPLES OF NUMERICAL FEATURES IN THE NAMES OF THE BIBLE WRITERS

The Bible writers' names are widely separated throughout the Scripture. It is remarkable to note that the number seven is found even in the scattered occurrences of these names.

Twenty-six writers are named in the Bible. There were others who wrote books of the Bible. However, only twenty-six of the writers are actually named in the Bible itself.

Of course, each of these twenty-six names, like all other Hebrew and Greek words, has a numeric value. In the following list the numeric value is placed beside each name.

Moses	345	Haggai	21
Isaiah	401	Zechariah	242
Jeremiah	271	Malachi	101
Ezekiel	156	David	14
Hosea	381	Solomon	375
Joel	47	Daniel	95
Amos	176	Ezra	278
Obadiah	91	Nehemiah	113
Jonah	71	James	833
Micah	75	Peter	755
Nahum	104	Jude	685
Habakkuk	216	Paul	781
Zephaniah	235	John	1069
		Total	7931

The following are a few examples of the many amazing numeric features which occur beneath the surface of these 26 names.

FEATURE ONE

The total numeric value of the Hebrew and Greek names of these 26 Bible writers is exactly ....7,931 or 1,133   7's

FEATURE TWO

The numeric value of the Hebrew name, Moses, writer of the first book, Genesis, and the numeric value of the Greek name, John, writer of the last book Revelation, is 345 and 1,069 respectively, which equals exactly ....1,414 or 202 7's
The other names have a numeric value of ....6,517 or 931 7's

FEATURE THREE

Of these 26 writers named in the Bible, the number of Old Testament writers named is exactly ....21 or 3 7's

FEATURE FOUR

The numeric value of the Hebrew names of the 21 Old Testament writers is exactly ....3,808 or 544 7's
The numeric value of the Greek names of the 5 New Testament writers is exactly ....4,123 or 589 7's

FEATURE FIVE

The numeric value of the 21 Old Testament writers, 3,808, is thus divided. The writers of the Law and Prophets (from Moses to Malachi— list of names above) have a numeric value of ....2,933 or 419 7's

The writers of the Hag-
iographa, (from David to
Nehemiah — list of names
above) have a numeric value
of ....875 or 125 7's

FEATURE SIX

Of the 21 Old Testament
writers, those named in the
New Testament are Moses,
David, Isaiah, Jeremiah, Dan-
iel, Hosea, Joel. In all exactly...........7

FEATURE SEVEN

The numeric value of these
seven names is exactly ....1,554 or 222 7's

FEATURE EIGHT

The number of times these
seven names occur in the
Old Testament is exactly ....2,310 or 330 7's

FEATURE NINE

Of these 2,310 occurrences of
the seven Bible writers' names
in the Old Testament, the
name which appears the
greatest number of times is
David. The number of times
his name is found is exactly ......1,134 or 162 7's

FEATURE TEN

The number of times the
name Moses, writer of the
first book, occurs is exactly ....847 or 121 7's
In this name Moses there
are 38 or more profound
numeric features.

All this seems so amazing—and so exhaustive—yet
the truth of the matter is, these are merely a few examples of the many astounding numerical features
which occur in the structure of these Bible writers'
names.

The above are examples of features which are not
confined to **single passages but** are examples of features which occur in the structure of special words—
words which are separated by great distances, appearing in many different parts and many different books
of the Bible. The reader can well understand that the
discovery of numerical features such as these requires
careful searching throughout the entire Scripture. Following is another illustration of numerical features
which occur in this same manner.

WORDS WHICH BEGIN AND END THE NEW TESTAMENT BOOKS

There are twenty-seven books in the New Testament. Thus there are twenty-seven words which begin these books and twenty-seven words which end
them, a total of fifty-four words.

The total numeric value of
these 54 Greek words which
begin and end the 27 books
of the New Testament is
exactly ....46,949 or 6,707   7's

This again is only one of the dozens of amazing numerical features which occur in the structure of these words. The reader will agree that features such as this one are indeed deeply and peculiarly hidden beneath the surface, and would not be discovered by mere readers of the Greek text, unless special investigation and calculations were made.

The following are other examples of features which underlie the surface of special words — words which are separated by great distances, appearing in many different books of the Bible.

FEATURE ONE
The Greek word "aionios"
(eternal) has a numeric value
of exactly ....1,141 or   163   7's

FEATURE TWO
This word is formed by adding "ios" to the noun "aion."
The noun "aion" has a nu-
meric value of exactly ....861 or   123   7's
The ending "ios" has a nu-
meric value of ....280 or   40   7's

FEATURE THREE
The number of times this
word occurs in the New
Testament is exactly ....70 or   10   7's

FEATURE FOUR
The numeric value of the
seventy occurrences of this
word is exactly ....76,783 or 10,969 7's

FEATURE FIVE
The singular forms have a
total numeric value of exactly..67,893 or 9,699 7's
The plural forms have a
total numeric value of exactly ..8,890 or 1,270 7's

The features enumerated above by no means form the complete list of numerical features which are strangely hidden in the occurrences of these words.

Similar features underlie the occurrences of thousands of other words. For example, the word "year" is distributed throughout the book of Genesis in such a marvelous manner that more than 20 amazing numeric features occur.

Thus far the reader has seen two distinct ways in which the number seven has been discovered in the structure of the original Bible text. Numerical features occur beneath the surface of **single passages** and also beneath the surface of special words which are separated by great distances appearing throughout the Bible.

Numerical features are peculiarly hidden in the structure of the original Bible text in dozens of other interesting and amazing manners. One other way in which the number seven occurs is briefly pointed out, then it will be explained how these amazing newly discovered numerical facts scientifically prove that the Bible is a supernatural, God inspired, God given book.

It is interesting to note that even the Bible as a whole divides perfectly into exactly seven great divisions.

1. The Law
2. The Prophets
3. The Writings (Hagiographa)
4. The Gospels
5. The Acts
6. The Epistles
7. Revelation

The two larger divisions, the Prophets and the Epistles, are each composed of a number of books which divides perfectly by seven. The number of books in each of these divisions is exactly 21, or 3 7's. There are dozens of other amazing numeric features strangely hidden beneath the surface of these seven Bible divisions.

CHAPTER FIVE

How Do The Newly Discovered Facts Scientifically Prove That The Bible Is A Supernatural, God Inspired Book?

The presence of the amazing numerical features or facts beneath the very surface of the original Bible text cannot be denied by anyone. There are actually thousands of phenomenal, numerical facts in the very structure of the Bible. One can ignore them and turn his eyes from them but the astounding numeric facts continue to be there. Our own opinions, likes or dislikes do not alter the facts in the least. Welcome or unwelcome, acknowledged or unacknowledged, the facts continue to be there. Their presence is one truth which every person must accept.

Now then, since these facts are actually found in the very structure of the Bible text, a certain logical question arises—

HOW CAN ONE ACCOUNT FOR THE PRESENCE OF THESE FACTS?

How did these features occur or come to be in the very structure of the Bible text? Their presence must be explained in some satisfactory way.

The reader will agree that there are only two possible ways in which these amazing facts could have occurred. They could have occurred either **by accident,** that is, by sheer chance, or **by design.** They could have occurred accidentally, or they could have been purposely designed or arranged—their occurrence in such a marvelous manner could have been planned and intended.

No doubt some are of the opinion that these features occurred accidentally—that they occurred in this peculiar manner merely by sheer chance. Now then—

WHAT ARE THE CHANCES FOR TWENTY-FOUR FEATURES TO OCCUR ACCIDENTALLY?

Suppose there are twenty-four numerical features or facts in the structure of a certain passage. What chances are there that these features would occur together in one passage accidentally? This is easily calculated, for there is a standard, recognized, scientific method of calculating chances — there is an established law of chances.

Only one number in seven is a multiple of seven. The other six numbers which are not multiples of seven have as good a chance to occur accidentally as the one that is a multiple of seven.

Therefore,

According to the law of chances,
　　for any 1 number to be a multiple of 7
　　accidentally, there is only one chance in 7

According to the law of chances,
　　for any 2 numbers to be multiples of 7 acci-
　　dentally, there is only one chance in 7 x 7,
　　or only one chance in 49

According to the law of chances,
　　for any 3 numbers to be multiples of 7
　　accidentally, there is only one chance in
　　7 x 49, or only one chance in 343

(The calculation continues on the same basis)

Thus, according to the law of chances,
　　for any 1 feature or numerical fact to occur
　　accidentally, there is only one chance in..................7

According to the law of chances,
　　for any 2 features or numerical facts to
　　occur accidentally, there is only one chance in
　　7 x 7, or only one chance in 49

According to the law of chances,
　　for any 3 features or numerical facts to occur
　　accidentally, there is only one chance in
　　7 x 49, or only one chance in 343

The chart below continues the calculation to the chance of 24 features occurring in a passage accidentally. The first three are repeated to include them with the others.

In place of the asterisk (*) substitute the words which are marked with the asterisk at the bottom of the chart.

For 1 feature * 1 chance in..7
For 2 features * 1 chance in...49
For 3 features * 1 chance in 343
For 4 features * 1 chance in..2,401
For 5 features * 1 chance in..16,807
For 6 features * 1 chance in 117,649
For 7 features * 1 chance in.......................................823,543
For 8 features * 1 chance in....................................5,764,801
For 9 features * 1 chance in................................40,353,607
For 10 features * 1 chance in.............................282,475,249
For 11 features * 1 chance in..........................1,977,326,743
For 12 features * 1 chance in.......................13,841,287,201
For 13 features * 1 chance in.....................96,889,010,407
For 14 features * 1 chance in...................678,223,072,849
For 15 features * 1 chance in................4,747,561,509,943
For 16 features * 1 chance in.............33,232,930,569,601
For 17 features * 1 chance in............232,630,513,987,207
For 18 features * 1 chance in..........1,628,413,597,910,449
For 19 features * 1 chance in........11,398,895,185,373,143
For 20 features * 1 chance in.........79,792,266,297,612,001
For 21 features * 1 chance in........558,545,864,083,284,007
For 22 features * 1 chance in.....3,909,821,048,582,988,049
For 23 features * 1 chance in...27,368,747,340,080,916,343
For 24 features * 1 chance in.191,581,231,380,566,414,401
      * "to occur accidentally, there is only"

Thus, according to the law of chances, for 24
features to occur in a passage accidentally, there is only
one chance in 191,581,231,380,566,414,401—only one
chance in one hundred ninety-one quintillion, five
hundred eighty-one quadrillion, two hundred thirty-one
trillion, three hundred eighty billion, five hundred sixty-
six million, four hundred fourteen thousand, four hundred one. *

Many brief Bible passages have as many as seventy
or a hundred or more amazing numeric features in
the very structure of their text. If there is only one
chance in quintillions that 24 features could occur together accidentally, what would the chance be for 70
features to occur together accidentally?

When there is only one chance in thousands for
something to happen accidentally, it is already considered highly improbable that it will occur at all.
When there is only one chance in hundreds of thousands, it is considered practically impossible. But here
there is one chance in not only millions, but
billions, and trillions, and quadrillions, and quintillions,
that merely 24 features could occur together in a passage accidentally.

The argument and demonstration is convincing
enough. The amazing numerical features of even one
small passage, to say nothing of the thousands in the
entire Bible, could not possibly have occurred by accident—by sheer chance. All this evidence simply can-

*The nomenclature herein used is the American,
not the British.

not be explained by the doctrine of chances. If these features did not occur accidentally, then there is only one conclusion, one alternative. They were purposely designed or arranged—their occurrence in such a mar' velous and mysterious manner was intended or planned.

The point can be illustrated in the following way:

Suppose for example, someone O O O O were carrying a bag which contained O O O O 24 oranges. Suppose that suddenly O O O O the bag broke and the 24 oranges fell O O O O to the floor. What chance would O O O O there be that the oranges would fall O O O O into four perfect rows with six in each row, each orange being exactly opposite the other? Such self arrangement would be considered impossible!

Suppose on the other hand you came into the room and found the oranges arranged in the manner described. You would come to only one conclusion, namely, that they were purposely designed or arranged in that unusual manner. No one would risk being called insane by insisting that such a thing occurred accidentally!

Likewise, these profound numeric features found in the very structure of the original Bible text are not there by sheer chance or accident, but by design. They are arranged according to definite plan; they form thousands of perfect and uniform designs.

It has been conclusively shown that there are amazing numerical features in the very structure of the Bible—their presence cannot be denied, but is a truth which everyone must accept. It has been proved that these features could not possibly have occurred by sheer chance or accident, but that they were arranged or designed. This is a second truth which everyone must accept.

Since the discovery of a design is proof of a designer, the next logical question arises—

WHO PLANNED AND CARRIED OUT THESE AMAZING NUMERIC DESIGNS?

Who caused them to occur in the very structure of the Bible text?

The thousands of perfect patterns and designs came into the Scripture through some intelligence. The reader will agree that there are only two possible intelligences that could have planned and brought about these profound designs. They could have come into the Scripture either by human intelligence or by superhuman, namely, divine intelligence.

Were these amazing numeric designs planned by the men who wrote the books of the Bible?

(1) The profound numeric patterns in the structure of the Bible passages could not possibly have been planned and worked out by mere human beings alone.

If anyone could write an intelligible passage of 300 words, constructing it in such a way that the same designs and schemes of sevens occur in the structure of its text as those found in the first seventeen verses of Matthew, indeed he would prove himself a wonder if he could accomplish it in six months. (Chapter 3)

If anyone could write an intelligible passage of 161 words, constructing it in such a manner that the same designs and arrangements of sevens occur in the structure of its text as those which are found in verses 18-25 of the first chapter of Matthew, he would accomplish a still greater wonder if he were able to do it in three years. (Chapter 3.)

If anyone in an entire lifetime of continuous work could write an intelligible passage of some 500 words, containing in its structure as many intertwined yet harmonious numeric features as are found in the second chapter of Matthew, it would be a miracle of miracles. (Chapter 3.)

No mortal in the lifetime of a hundred years could possibly have carried out the design which is found in even a single book of the Bible, if he devoted the entire hundred years to the task. It would require some centuries to write a book designed and constructed in the manner in which the book of Matthew is constructed.

It must be remembered that with each additional sentence the difficulty of constructing these numerical features increases not only in arithmetical progression, but in geometrical progression, for each paragraph is designed so as to develop constantly fixed numeric relations to the material which precedes and follows it. Every additional letter, word, and sentence makes the matter tremendously more complicated and comprehensive.

The reader must also observe that many of the Scripture writers were men chosen from very ordinary walks of life—men who had little or no schooling at all. If Matthew, Mark, Luke or John, for instance, had attempted to construct and produce the harmonious numeric features and designs which are found in their books as a whole, and had attempted to produce separate numeric schemes and designs which occur in each division, and in each sub-division, and in the words, forms, vocabularies, letters, etc., how long would it have taken them to construct their books? Centuries upon centuries!

Certainly, mere human beings alone could not possibly have planned and worked out the amazing designs of numeric features which occur in the very structure of the Bible text. The limitations of the human intellect and the shortness of human life make it impossible for any man or any set of men combined to accomplish such stupendous feats.

Dr. D. B. Turney tells how he attempted to construct a passage that would show some numeric features. He declares, "I gave numeric values to the English alphabet, and tried to prepare a passage which would adhere to the numerics, and make every section a multiple of seven, and present all the other features of Biblical arithmography, without letting the meaning of the passage descend to nonsense. After working thereon for days, I could get no satisfaction. Yet this feature is accomplished in every one of the thousands of Bible paragraphs without the slightest visible effort."

(2) The marvelous numeric designs which extend over many books of the Bible could not possibly have been planned and carried out by the writers themselves.

Not only are the phenomenal designs confined to the text of single Bible passages, but **widely separated portions** of the Bible are woven into intricate and perfect patterns. Special words which are scattered through many different books of the Bible form amaz- ing chain-designs that literally teem with numerical features. The numeric designs in the structure of the Bible writers' names were given as examples of these word-chains which extend throughout the entire Scrip- tures. (Chapter Four) The discovery of such designs requires careful searching in all parts of the 66 books of the Bible.

The double design of sevens in the name "Moses," for example, could not, have been planned and carried out by the Bible writers themselves. It must be remembered that the writers did not live at the same time—they lived many years apart. In fact there was a period of about 1600 years between the writing of the first book of the Bible and the last. It must be remembered also that the 66 books were written by 33 different persons. And it must be remem- bered that these persons were scattered throughout various countries of the world and that they were men of widely different backgrounds. Many of the writers had little or no schooling. How could these men have planned the distribution of the name "Moses" throughout the entire Bible so as to form marvelous numeric designs?

How could each one of the 33 writers who lived in various countries, the last writer separated by 1600 years from the first, insert the name "Moses" just enough times to keep the numeric design in suspense until it came to John, the last writer who used it in the book of Revelation just once to complete the design? How could each writer have known that he should use a particular word a certain number of times so that when all would be finished after 1600 years the total would divide perfectly by seven and would show numeric design? Certainly such design could not possibly have been planned by the writers themselves. The case of Moses is only one example of a chain design which extends throughout the entire Bible. Literally hundreds of other cases as convincing as this can be pointed out.

Each word of the whole Scripture is linked and connected in one marvelous pattern. All the intricacies and beauties of the separate and smaller patterns when put together form one great design. Thus the entire Bible is tied together by a continuous pattern from Genesis to Revelation.

The designs interlock paragraph with paragraph, book with book, and the Old Testament with the New Testament. The numerics of the Old Testament and those of the New together form harmonious schemes which could not be made possible or solved without either of the Testaments. The Old Testament was concluded 400 years before the New Testament was begun, yet the two when taken together form one complete revelation. Both accord perfectly—both are parts of one homogeneous whole.

The fact that the Bible was written by a number of different persons in various countries of the world over a period of hundreds of years makes it impossible for the writers to have planned these patterns Designs which cover some 1600 years could never have been planned and carried out by man, for many of the words were penned without any knowledge of what would be written by other writers many years later. Even if it were possible for the 33 different writers to meet and confer about the use of their vocabularies, etc., it would require thousands of years to carry out such profound numeric schemes.

The minds of the cleverest men who have ever lived would not be capable of devising such sublime mathematical problems. No human minds could possibly have devised such a means of binding the whole of the Word together.

(3) The special elaborate numeric designs in each book of the Bible could not possibly have been planned and carried out by the writers unaided.

The number of words found in Matthew, not found in any of the other 26 New Testament books, shows elaborate designs. How did Matthew know that he should use certain words which would not be used in any of the other 26 books of the New Testament? In order for him to have done this it would have been necessary for him to have had all these other books before him as he wrote his book. If he had all these other 26 books before him as he wrote, it would mean that he wrote his Gospel last.

It so happens, however, that each of the other books has a certain number of words which are not found in any other New Testament book. These words show phenomenal numeric designs. How did each writer know that he should use a certain number of words which would not be used in any other book? In order for each writer to have done this it would have been necessary for each one to have had all the other 26 books before him as he wrote. If each had the other 26 books before him as he wrote it would mean that each particular Gospel was written last. But such a thing is an utter impossibility! How could each Gospel writer have the other 26 books before him as he wrote? Such a thing is unthinkable!

These are only a few of the many problems which confront a person who tries to figure out how mere men could have designed and arranged the phenomenal numeric features in the structure of the original Bible text. Certainly these amazing numerical designs could not possibly have been planned and carried out by mere human beings.

It is interesting to note that as far as is known,

THE BIBLE IS THE ONLY BOOK IN EXISTENCE WHICH IS CONSTRUCTED ON AN AMAZING NUMERIC DESIGN

At first glance the most obvious objection to the numeric features of the Bible is that such or similar numerics could be extracted from any other writings in any language if sufficient time and ingenuity were expended. However, this is not the case. The Bible

is different from all other books. No other piece of
literature anywhere in the entire world is known to
contain amazing numerical features such as are found
in the structure of the Bible text. The Apocrapha
shows no evidence of such numeric design. Various persons have devoted much time to the examination of the
Greek classics in an effort to find the same mathematical structure, but no such phenomena have yet been
found anywhere.

Various professors of Greek have been requested
to submit Greek prose classics to the numeric test to
ascertain if this same amazing numerical phenomena
could be found. No one has reported any success in
finding such numeric designs.

No human beings could have written the Bible
in the way it is demonstrated to have been written.
No human foresight or arrangement could have secured
such results beforehand; no human powers could have
carried them out to such perfection. Man by his own
attainments could not perform such unthinkable feats.
It is simply impossible to account for these designs of
numeric features if the mere human authorship of the
Bible is assumed.

If human logic is worth anything at all we are
simply driven to the conclusion that the thousands of
amazing numeric designs in the very structure of the
original Bible text could not possibly have been planned by the men who wrote the books of the Bible—
they could never have been produced by mere human
minds.

It is evident that the Bible is not the work of many minds, but the work of One Mind. The designs furnish clear proof that the whole Bible has but one Author. All the books of both the Old and New Testaments were planned and produced by the same Mind.

Every candid, logical minded individual is simply compelled to admit that the intelligence which planned and designed the Bible must have been Superhuman, Divine. That One Designer was a Supernatural, Master Designer. Only the Supreme, Omniscient, Omnipotent God could have caused such phenomenal numeric designs to occur beneath the surface of the Bible text. Only God could have constructed the Bible in the amazing manner in which it is constructed. The Eternal, Omnipotent Author designed, superintended, worked, and carried out His Own infinite plans. There is no escape from this conclusion.

Thus the newly discovered designs of numerical features or facts scientifically prove that the great Bible claim concerning itself (Chapter One) is actually true. The Bible actually is a supernatural, God inspired, God given book as it claims to be, for mere human beings alone could not possibly have written and constructed it in the marvelous manner in which it is constructed.

Indeed, "all scripture" is "God breathed." The words which the writers of the Bible recorded were not their own words, but were the very words of God Himself—they wrote only as they were "moved" or "in-breathed" by the Spirit of God.

The newly discovered designs of numerical facts in the very structure of the text mathematically prove the divine verbal and literal inspiration of the Scrip-tures. There is no need to explain and discuss the numerous theories of inspiration, for the divine verbal and literal inspiration of the Scriptures is not a mere "theory," but an actual "fact." We have before our very eyes an actual scientific demonstration of the divine verbal inspiration of the Bible.

In geometry the two angles at the base of an isosceles triangle are proved to be equal by cold un-impassioned mathematical reasoning about which there can be no dispute. So the divine inspiration of the Bible is proved with all the clearness and positiveness of mathematical precision. Skeptics can bring no indictment against the proof made possible by the numerical facts, for the proof deals with mathematical certainties. The modern scientific method, the hard logic, the sound laws of reasoning, are astounding. One cannot argue with mathematics for it is an exact science.

The facts are undeniable and indisputable—their conclusions are unavoidable. They are stupendous, overwhelming evidences of divine inspiration which shatter all the arguments of non-believers.

The discoveries of facts as important as these, are indeed "Astounding New Discoveries." They are as amazing as any discoveries that could be made. The results are staggering. The facts are hardly con-ceivable except that they are visible before our eyes. One is forced to say with awe, "This is the work of

God Himself." God has written His signature in His Word in this phenomenal manner so that no man can claim it as a human production.

The very nature of the newly discovered facts is such that an intelligent, unbiased, rational person cannot deny the convincing demonstration. The mind of a person is so constructed that when he is brought face to face with certain facts, regardless of how unwelcome they might be, he is simply compelled to admit that the results are so. When it is demonstrated that A equals B and that B equals C, he must draw the conclusion that A also equals C. He may dislike the conclusion, he may find it costly, but he must acknowledge the result.

It is utterly foolish for anyone to say that the numerical facts do not underlie the actual text and vocabulary of the Bible passages. They are there! To make such a statement would be as foolish as saying that there is no blood in a living human being.

The evidences and facts are such that no destructive critic can successfully face them. Facing them means unconditional surrender to the inevitable. They form an unanswerable argument—they make possible a certain and foolproof system which can stand any amount of honest testing. No living person has yet attempted to dispute this convincing array of facts. The best anyone can do is to ignore them.

Robert Ingersoll, the noted infidel lecturer, was continually crying for a miracle. Here are hundreds of miracles! Let anyone deal with these facts and show how they occurred in the very structure of the original Bible text if they did not occur in a miraculous way!

CHAPTER SIX

Two Supremely Important Questions Now Definitely Settled By The Newly Discovered Facts

The amazing newly discovered facts forever settle the following two important questions regarding the Bible.

Throughout the years there has been great controversy over the question whether the Bible is actually a supernatural God inspired book as it claims it is, or whether it is a book purely of human origin—the writings of mere men without any divine influence whatsoever. This question has now been definitely settled beyond all speculation, for the profound facts discovered beneath the very surface of the original Bible text scientifically prove that the Bible could not possibly have been written by mere human beings alone, but that it is a supernatural, God given book. Any unbiased, open-minded person who is willing to face the facts will agree to this. Thus the facts definitely settle this first question.

There is, however, another great question which has arisen in regard to the Bible. The newly discovered facts in an amazing and marvelous manner also definitely settle this question. Before it can be discussed, it is first necessary to inform or remind the reader of the following subject matter which has a direct bearing on the question to be considered.

THE ORIGINAL MANUSCRIPTS WHICH THE BIBLE WRITERS THEMSELVES WROTE, HAVE BEEN LOST

So far as is known, none of the original manuscripts are now in existence. It is certain, however, that God could have caused them to have been preserved if it were His will to do so. There seems to be a reason why these original manuscripts were not preserved.

Why Did God Allow the Original Manuscripts To Disappear?

If the original manuscripts were available they might have been worshiped. Many human beings are ready to worship anything which lays any claim to sanctity. Bones and ashes of saints, splinters said to be from the cross upon which Christ hung, bits of linen cloth said to have been worn by Jesus, by the Virgin Mary, or by some venerated saint, nails from the crosses upon which martyrs hung, clothing, furniture, all these and more have been worshiped by many. In the book of II Kings 18:4 Hezekiah was commanded to destroy the brazen serpent made by Moses because it was worshiped. If the original handwriting of Moses, David, Paul, or other Bible writers should now exist, there would no doubt be many who would worship it, and thus detract from the worship of the invisible God.

Furthermore, the preservation of the original manuscripts was quite unnecessary for there exists such an abundance of good manuscript copies, ancient versions or translations, paraphrases, quotations, commentaries, harmonies, accounts, lists, etc.

Thus the Old Testament and New Testament manuscripts which are available today are ancient copies of the originals.

There are a number of important Hebrew manuscript copies which contain the complete Old Testament. In addition to these, there are partially complete, and fragmentary manuscripts which make a total of about 1,700. There are also about 350 copies of the ancient Septuagint version or translation, besides copies of many other translations of the Hebrew Old Testament.

There are more than 4,000 Greek manuscript copies of the New Testament. In addition to these there are about 8,000 manuscripts of the Latin Vulgate translation and at least 1,000 manuscripts of other ancient translations. Thus there are more than 13,000 manuscript copies of the whole or parts of the New Testament.

If every ancient manuscript copy and every modern printed copy of the New Testament were destroyed, the entire New Testament, with the exception of eleven verses could be reproduced from the thousands of quotations which are clearly found in the writings of the early Christians. During the first centuries, Christians in their writings quoted New Testament verses and passages so frequently that prac' tically the entire Testament could be reproduced by merely referring to these writings.

The reader's attention is called to the fact that there are a number of passages in the New Testament which have been seriously disputed by scholars. An example of such a passage is the last twelve verses in the Gospel of Mark—Mark 16:9-20. The reader may be surprised to learn that this passage is **not** found in some of the ancient manuscript copies of the New Testament. However, it is found in many of the other manuscript copies.

When preparing editions of the Greek New Tes' tament and translations of it, scholars have had to decide which set of copies they would follow. Should they follow the ancient New Testament manuscript copies which include this particular passage or the copies which do not include it? Which set of copies is correct on this particular issue? A question of this kind naturally has caused great controversy. Some insist that the passage should be included while others contend the opposite. Those who reject the passage maintain that it is merely a passage which someone has written of his own initiative and has inserted or added to the God inspired manuscript.

They naturally declare that such passages if they are foreign or new material should not be included in the inspired Bible as the very word of God, but should be marked or designated in some way as the writings of human origin, or eliminated altogether. Such passages are said to be "interpolations"—foreign or new material inserted into the original words of the Author.

There are twelve such passages in the New Testa-ment which are said by some to be interpolations. The passages are found in some manuscripts, but not found in others. Which copies should translators follow? Which copies give the true and original text? Are the passages genuine portions of God's Word or are they man's addition to it?

If the original parchments upon which the apostles wrote their books were available, a question of this kind would not arise, for New Testament translators would have before them the apostles' original hand-written text. However, as it is, scholars can refer only to ancient copies of the original parchments—copies which disagree in regard to 12 passages in particular. They have had to decide which manuscripts give the true original text—the copies which contain certain passages, or the copies which do not contain them.

The newly discovered facts, in a marvelous and amazing manner, definitely settle the question over a disputed passage. This is the second great question which the newly discovered facts definitely settle—the question whether certain passages actually belong in the divinely inspired Bible or whether they are pas-sages of human origin which someone has inserted into the inspired text.

An example is the passage which has already been mentioned, namely:

THE BOOK OF MARK, CHAPTER SIXTEEN VERSES 9-20

The Last Twelve Verses Of Mark

Are the last twelve verses of Mark's Gospel a genuine portion of the divinely inspired Bible, or are they an "interpolation?"

This question has been disputed by many scholars throughout the years. Some of the best editors of the Greek New Testament consider that this passage of twelve verses is an "interpolation." They honestly believe that it is foreign or new material which some-one has added to the original, inspired Bible. Perhaps no other passage in the entire Bible has been disputed more than this one.

Some of the foremost editors of the Greek New Testament have treated the passage as follows: Weiss places these verses in the margin. Tregelles and Alford retain them, but not as a genuine portion of Mark. Tischendorff omits them altogether. The revisers of 1881 separate them from the rest of the Gospel by an unusual space.

Westcott and Hort, perhaps by far the best equipped and most nearly correct editors of the Greek New Testament, mark these verses in double brackets, designating that in their honest judgment the verses do not belong in the New Testament and are an "interpolation."

Westcott and Hort were godly men who loved the Bible. After twenty-eight years of conscientious work in comparing manuscripts and editing the Greek New Testament, they came to the conclusion that the last twelve verses were not part of the Word of God. The reason for this is that Westcott and Hort based all their work principally on the Vatican and Sinai Manuscripts. These are the two oldest manuscripts and they decided that the disputed reading of a passage should generally be settled whenever these two manuscripts agree. Now it so happens that neither of these two manuscripts contains the last twelve verses of Mark, but hundreds of other manuscript copies do contain them.

The reader can thus well understand why these verses have been a matter of dispute among theologians.

Are the last twelve verses of Mark's Gospel a genuine portion of the Word of God or are they an "interpolation?"

Does the passage contain amazing numerical features beneath the surface of its text? Do the same divine marks which occur in the structure of genuine Bible passages occur in this particular passage? The answer is, yes! The passage is constructed on an elaborate **numerical design**—a design which could not possibly have originated with man. The scores of numerical facts which lie beneath the surface of its text, prove that it is a genuine, supernatural, God inspired portion of the Bible.

The following are a few examples of the many numerical features discovered in the very structure of this passage.

FEATURE ONE
The number of Greek words
in the last 12 verses of Mark
is exactly ....175 or · 25   7's

FEATURE TWO

The number of vocabulary
words in the passage is
exactly ....98 or 14 7's

FEATURE THREE

The number of nouns in the
98 vocabulary words is exactly........21 or 3 7's
Of these 98 Greek vocabulary
words, the number which are
not nouns is ....77 or 11 7's

FEATURE FOUR

Of the 21 nouns, the number
which begin with a con-
sonant is exactly ....14 or 2 7's
Of the 21 nouns, the number
that begin with a vowel is 7

FEATURE FIVE

The number of Greek letters
in the 98 vocabulary words is
exactly ....553 or 79 7's

FEATURE SIX

Of these 553 letters, the
number of vowels is ....294 or 42 7's
Of these 553 letters, the
number of consonants is
exactly ....259 or 37 7's

FEATURE SEVEN

The number of forms is
exactly ....133 or 19 7's

FEATURE EIGHT
The numeric value of the 133
forms is exactly ....89,663 or 12,809   7's

FEATURE NINE
Of these 133 forms, the number which occur only once
is exactly 112   or   16   7's
The number of those which
occur more than once is 21   or   3   7's

FEATURE TEN
Of the 98 vocabulary words,
the number of words used in
passages which precede this
particular passage in the Gos-
pel of Mark is exactly 84   or   12   7's
The number of words not
found in the preceding passages of Mark but found here
for the first time is exactly 14   or   2   7's

FEATURE ELEVEN
Of these 98 Greek vocabulary
words, the number used by
Christ in addressing His dis-
ciples is exactly 42   or   6   7's
The number of vocabulary
words which form no part of
Christ's speech is 56   or   8   7's

FEATURE TWELVE
Of the 175 Greek words in
the entire passage, the number used by Christ in His
speech is exactly 56   or   8   7's

Of these 175 words, the
number that form no part
of Christ's speech is 119   or   17   7's

The 12 verses (Mark 16:9-20) divide themselves into—

THREE NATURAL DIVISIONS

Verses 9-11 form Division A.
Verses 12-18 form Division B.
Verses 19-20 form Division C.

The amazing features found in the passage as a
whole are also found in each of its three natural
divisions.

DIVISION A. (Verses 9-11)

FEATURE THIRTEEN

The number of Greek words
in this Division — (Verses
9, 10, 11) is 35   or   5   7's

FEATURE FOURTEEN
The numeric value of this
division is 17,213   or   2,459   7's

FEATURE FIFTEEN
The numeric value of verses
9 and 11 is exactly 11,795   or   1,685   7's
The numeric value of verse
10 is 5,418   or   774   7's

FEATURE SIXTEEN

The first Greek word in verse
10 has a numeric value of
exactly 98   or   14   7's

FEATURE SEVENTEEN

The last Greek word in verse
10 has a numeric value of
exactly 791   or   113   7's
The remaining words in verse
10 have a numeric value of 4,529   or   647   7's

FEATURE EIGHTEEN

Of the 35 Greek words in
Division A (verses 9, 10, 11)
the number which begin with
a vowel is exactly 14   or   2   7's
The number of words which
begin with a consonant is 21   or   3   7's

FEATURE NINETEEN

Of the 35 Greek words in
this Division, the number
that end with a vowel is
exactly 21   or   3   7's
The number of words that
end with a consonant is 14   or   2   7's

FEATURE TWENTY

The number of syllables in
the 35 Greek words of Divis-
ion A is exactly 84   or   12   7's

This by no means exhausts the interesting numerical features of Division A. These same features and many more are repeated in Divisions B. and C. In order not to weary the reader with countless numerical features, just one feature from each of these two divisions is given below.

DIVISION B. (Verses 12-18)

FEATURE TWENTY-ONE
The number of Greek words
in Division B is 105   or   15   7s'

DIVISION C. (Verses 19-20)

FEATURE TWENTY-TWO
The number of Greek words
in Division C is 35   or   5   7's

FEATURE TWENTY-THREE
Of special interest is the fact
that these last twelve verses
of Mark have just one word
which is found nowhere else
in the New Testament. It is
the word "thanasimos" which
means "deadly." The numeric
value of this word is exactly..........581   or   83   7's
This one word in itself has
no less than seven amazing
features.

This passage not only shows an amazing design as a whole but it shows designs within the design, and further designs within those. The separate paragraphs have designs of their own within the design. The vocabulary has its design, and the forms have theirs. It is marvelous indeed!

The above 23 amazing numeric facts or features are merely examples of those which occur beneath the surface of the 175 words in the last twelve verses of Mark. There are a hundred or more astounding features in the very structure of this passage. It is needless to weary the reader with further enumeration of the numeric phenomena.

According to the law of chances (calculation chart in the preceding chapter) there is only one chance in 27,368,747,340,080,916,343 that these 23 features of sevens could occur together in one passage accidentally. If the number is this high for merely 23 features, what chance would there be for 70 or 100 features to occur together accidentally?

Not only is there an abundance of numerical facts and designs hidden beneath the surface of the passage itself, but certain words in the passage are parts of elaborate designs which extend to many other books of the New Testament. For example, the word "baptizo" (baptize) which occurs in these last twelve verses of Mark is part of a numeric design that runs through all the New Testament passages in which this word occurs. There are some 20 amazing features in the design through the word "baptizo"—a design which is composed of widely separated occurrences of the word in different books of the Bible. If this particular passage were to be torn from the Scripture, there would be one less occurrence of this word "baptizo," and the entire New Testament design through this word would be utterly destroyed. Many other words in these last twelve verses of Mark are links in chains of features—are parts of designs which include other New Testament books. Without this passage the many elaborate numeric designs would be destroyed.

The demonstration is convincing enough. These numeric features did not occur in this passage by chance. They were designed to occur the way they do. Certainly the designs and features are beyond the ability of mere man to construct—they can only be attributed to God Himself. Thus the numerical facts discovered in the very structure of the passage definitely prove that it is not an "interpolation" of man, but that it is God's passage, and that it is entitled to its place in the divinely inspired Bible.

Thus, the numerical facts forever settle the question whether or not the passage is an interpolation.

It is true that these verses strangely disappeared from the two oldest manuscripts. How or why they disappeared we do not know. Some of the words are a strong condemnation of Satan. Could it be that he inspired someone to remove them—could it be that he sought to permanently banish them from the Scriptures? If such were the case it was merely an "attempt" which failed, for it is now definitely known that these verses are a genuine portion of God's Word.

Various scholars have declared that the following passage is an interpolation.

THE ACCOUNT OF THE WOMAN TAKEN IN ADULTERY—John 7:53 to 8:11

This passage is not found in some of the ancient manuscript copies of the New Testament. Scholars, when preparing their Greek editions and translations of the New Testament, have had to decide which manuscripts to follow. Should they follow copies which include the verses, or copies which do not include them? Which of the many manuscript copies give the true original text?

If the original parchment upon which John wrote his Gospel were available, a question of this kind would not arise because scholars would have before them John's own handwritten text. However, as it is, there are only copies of the original parchments available—copies which vary or differ in that some contain the verses while others do not contain them.

Westcott and Hort had no doubt in their minds whatever that this story was not part of the original text. They and many other able scholars have believed that when we read this passage in our Bibles, we are not reading the Word of God, but a passage which someone has added to it.

Editors have rejected this passage from the New Testament with even greater assurance than the last twelve verses of Mark. Tregelles, who was a strictly orthodox editor of the New Testament, and who believed as firmly in the divine inspiration of the Scriptures as anyone, honestly confessed that the account of the woman taken in adultery was not part of the Word of God. Various other scholars, on the contrary, have earnestly contended that the passage is entitled to its place in the Bible.

Is this a genuine God inspired passage or is it a passage of human origin which someone has added to the inspired Bible?

Does the passage contain the divine numerical designs beneath the surface of its text? Yes—the passage is permeated with the same phenomenal numeric designs and features as are found in the structure of genuine God inspired passages. The profound numeric features and schemes found therein could not possibly have originated with man. We definitely know that this passage is divinely inspired and that it is not to be erased or excluded from the Bible, or even disfigured by brackets.

It is true these verses strangely disappeared from the oldest manuscripts. However, various other manuscripts contain them. How or why they disappeared we do not know.

The following passage, which is very brief, yet very important, has been disputed by scholars.

CHRIST'S FIRST PRAYER FROM THE CROSS

"Father, forgive them; for they know not what they do."—Luke 23:34.

Some manuscript copies of the New Testament contain the verse while others do not. Which manuscript copies are correct on this point? Does this prayer rightfully belong in the God inspired Bible, or is it an interpolation by man?

Certainly we would like to know whether or not Christ actually uttered that prayer. Matters and questions of this nature are of vital importance to all true Christians. How could an earnest and sincere Christian rest in peace until he knew for certain whether passages such as these are genuine portions of God's Word or whether they are interpolations which should be torn out of the Bible?

Various editors consider that this brief prayer is an interpolation. However, it has now been discovered that the prayer is permeated with the same amazing numeric features found throughout genuinely inspired Bible passages. Thus, we have conclusive proof that this prayer is actually part of the inspired Bible—not an addition to it.

Christ uttered six other statements or cries from the cross. When this prayer is included, there are then exactly seven statements which Christ uttered from the cross.

CHRIST'S AGONY IN THE GARDEN

Luke 22:44

This account, which tells that Christ agonized in the garden to such an extent that he sweat great drops of blood, has also been disputed.

Is it a God inspired passage, or is it an interpolation?

The amazing numeric features contained in the very structure of the passage give sufficient and conclusive proof that the account did not originate with man, but that it is a divinely inspired passage, which rightfully belongs in the Bible.

In all, there are twelve such disputed passages in the New Testament which are definitely settled by these newly discovered facts.

CHAPTER SEVEN

Four Other Supremely Important Questions Now Definitely Settled By The Newly Discovered Facts

It has been shown in the preceding chapters that the newly discovered facts definitely settle two important questions—(1) the question whether the Bible is actually a God inspired book as it claims, or whether it is a mere human production, and (2) the question whether certain passages are genuine God inspired passages or whether they are mere human interpolations or additions to the inspired Bible.

But the amazing newly discovered numerical features do more than this—there are four other important questions which they definitely settle. Number (3) is—

THE QUESTION CONCERNING THE TRUE READING OF CERTAIN PASSAGES

There are two reasons in particular why it has been difficult at times to determine the correct reading of some passages. One reason is that the words in the oldest Hebrew and Greek manuscripts have no spaces between them, and there is very little punctuation. The separation of Hebrew and Greek words in some cases is a matter of mere editorial opinion. Thus at times editors differ as to which is the correct read- ing or interpretation of a passage.

As an illustration, consider the following English words written without any spaces between them.

Otherwisemenwoulddoit.

This could be read in either of two ways.

Other wise men would do it.
or
Otherwise, men would do it.

If the Bible had originally been written in English, and this sentence had been included in it without any spaces or punctuation, there might have been some lengthy theological discussions over the insertion or omission of a space between the words "other" and "wise."

The following words written without spaces is another illustration.

Godisnowhere.

This also could be read in either of two ways.

God is nowhere.
or
God is now here.

If the Bible had originally been written in English and this sentence were to occur, some atheist would probably foolishly insist that the true reading should be

"God is nowhere," while the theologian would contend that the correct reading should be "God is now here."

These illustrations in English help emphasize the fact that rendering the correct reading of a passage is indeed quite an important matter.

Thus one reason why it has been difficult at times to determine the correct reading of certain Bible passages is that there are no spaces between the words in the oldest Hebrew and Greek manuscripts. However, a far greater reason than this is that—

THE MANUSCRIPT COPIES VARY OR DIFFER SLIGHTLY

It has been stated that the original parchments or manuscripts upon which the Bible writers first wrote are not available, but that there is an abundance of good manuscript copies. The reader's attention is called to the fact that these copies give slightly different readings in some cases. These variations or different readings include such matters as differences in spelling, transposition of letters, words, and clauses, order of words, etc., which are the fault of the scribes or copyists. However, it must be remembered that the doctrine of the Bible or the article of faith is not affected in the least by these slight variations and only in a very few places is the actual sense of passages affected.

Why do the manuscript copies differ slightly in wording, spelling, etc.?

When the reader considers the laborious task of copying manuscripts by hand—especially manuscripts as large as the Old or New Testament—he will agree that it would be very easy to make errors in copying. A letter, a syllable, or a word could easily be omitted. Likewise, they could easily be transposed. One word could be mistaken for a similar word—for example, "proelthon" for "proselthon." Some letters are so sim-ilar they could be mistaken for another. Sometimes a change in a letter would mean a change in a word, especially in Hebrew. If the manuscripts were dictated, variations might be traced to the inaccurate or unalert hearing of the scribe, or to the poor pronunciation of the reader. Variations could also easily occur if the scribes carried long sentences or thoughts in their minds with-out referring to the manuscript from which they were copying.

Suppose someone should make a hand-written man-uscript of say 100 pages. Suppose 100 people should make copies by hand. How many errors or variations would there be? It is not easy to get copying done these days without variations. Suppose the work were done in the uncial or capital Greek letters without any spaces between the words, even by one who was familiar with that language. How many variations would occur?

It is worth while to note the pronounced contrast between the manner in which the Old Testament was copied and manner in which the New Testament was copied.

The Hebrew Old Testament was copied by official and professional scribes who worked under strict and stringent rules regarding pen, ink, parchment, length of page, line, etc. The copyists zealously watched over every detail of their work and the manuscripts were handled with great care. The divisions, words, and letters were carefully counted and recorded. If even one slight error were discovered in their work the entire scroll was discarded and a new one was made. Prayer was offered and pens were wiped after a certain number of words. Thus the work of copying was ceremoniously and religiously done and it conformed to a definite high standard of quality. Because of this extreme care on the part of expert scribes, the many Hebrew Old Testament manuscript copies do not vary or differ greatly regarding the reading of certain verses. The Hebrew Old Testament copies have come down to us with comparatively few variant or different readings.

The books of the Greek New Testament were frequently copied without such care. A person in the early Christian church who desired a copy of the New Testament books or letters could hire a professional scribe to do the work if he could afford to do so. This would insure a high degree of accuracy. If he could not afford to do so he could employ a cheaper and less capable copyist, or else he could do the work himself. This would mean work poorly done, and a copy containing variant readings. Often he would be a poor copyist and would not be interested in small details. He would be after the substance of the salvation message, not necessarily the exact words and forms. Thus the many New Testament Greek manuscript copies differ or vary in regard to the exact wording of certain verses more frequently than the Hebrew Old Testament manuscript copies do.

Thus the manuscripts through careless copying are defective in some passages—they differ more or less one from another. These differences however, as already stated, are for the most part very slight and in no case affect a single doctrine of the Bible.

When scholars and translators have prepared editions of the Bible in its original languages or translations of it, they have not always followed one particular manuscript copy, but they have had before them many copies of the text which they followed at times. Hundreds of manuscripts have been carefully compared and examined—their testimony has been carefully ascertained and duly weighed. The comparison of these manuscripts shows a uniformity and proves a common source.

The King James or Authorized version of the Bible, which is the most popular and best loved edition, was translated in the year 1611. At that time there were only about 2000 Greek copies of the New Testament text available for comparison, and they were not early copies, but were comparatively late in date. The 1611 translation was thus made from the Hebrew and Greek texts which were then available. However, since 1611 when this translation was made, scholars have found several thousand more manuscripts—some of which are better and are of earlier dates. Since the discovery of these better and earlier manuscripts, scholars saw that the wording of certain passages could be slightly changed. Thus in 1885 the well known Revised version was published. (The New Testament was completed and published in 1881. However it was not until 1885 that the revision of the Old Testament was completed.) Slight changes were made as to the wording of certain verses, etc. However, the meaning, the sense, and the doctrine of the Bible remained exactly the same.

In 1881 Dr. Westcott and Dr. Hort, two devout Christian men, published an edition of the Greek New Testament after they had spent 28 years carefully examining and comparing thousands of Greek New Testament manuscript copies, which as already stated differ or vary slightly in matters of spelling, order of words, transposition of words, clauses, etc. From all these Greek manuscript copies they gathered a text which scholars have considered to be one of the finest Greek New Testament texts ever printed. However, in their text they left numerous alternative readings. Each time they were not certain which one of two readings to follow, they placed one reading in the text and left the other in the margin as an alternative. The alternative reading could be substituted for the one in the text.

Thus the many scholars who have devoted years to editing particularly the New Testament have found it difficult at times to determine the exact reading of passages where ancient manuscripts differ. They have had to decide which of the many manuscripts they would follow on certain readings. Some have insisted that a verse should read as it appears in one certain manuscript and others have contended that it should read as it is found in a different manuscript. Questions concerning the correct reading of passages have naturally caused a great deal of controversy and dispute.

It has been pointed out that at times it has been difficult to determine the true reading of passages for two reasons—because there are no spaces between the words in the oldest Hebrew and Greek manuscripts and because of the variant or different readings in the many manuscripts.

The newly discovered facts, in an amazing and marvelous manner, definitely settle the dispute and question concerning the true reading of any Bible passage. They provide a positive test whereby the true and original text of Scripture may be ascertained beyond the possibility of doubt. The following is an example of a disputed reading from the Old Testament

BOOK OF ISAIAH, CHAPTER NINE, VERSE THREE

The American Revised Version follows certain manuscripts and gives the translation of the verse as follows:

"Thou hast multiplied the nations; thou **hast** increased their joy."

The Authorized or King James Version follows other manuscripts and translates the verse in the following manner:

"Thou hast multiplied the nations, and not increased their joy "

The American Revised Version tells that God **has** increased their joy, while the King James Version says that God **has not** increased their joy—a difference between yes and no. Which reading is correct?

In the Hebrew manuscript copies this is the difference of only one letter.

The newly discovered facts definitely settle the question. The Hebrew text of this passage which the Revised Version uses shows an elaborate design of numeric features. If even one letter of the verse is changed to another the entire numeric design fails. The Hebrew text of the passage from which the King James Version is translated shows no numerical design. Thus the newly discovered facts in the very structure of the passage definitely settle the question of the cor' rect reading. They prove that the Revised Version gives the correct reading.

Some may think a question of this nature does not make much difference any way. They may feel that it is not a matter of great importance. But, suppose the question had been about the statement "He that believeth on the Son **hath** life" or "He that believeth on the Son **hath not** life." This would have been a question of the utmost importance.

The following is an example of a disputed reading from the New Testament.

I CORINTHIANS, CHAPTER 13, VERSE 3

The amazing numerical design in the structure of the text also settles the correct reading of this disputed passage.

The Revised Version follows certain Greek Manuscript copies and gives the translation of one particular phrase of the verse as follows:

"if I give my body to be burned"

Wescott and Hort, in their Greek New Testament, follow other manuscripts and render the disputed portion differently. Instead of "if I give my body to be burned," they use **"if I give my body so that I may glory."**

In the Greek this is a difference of only one letter. Which is the correct reading?

The newly discovered facts in a marvelous manner settle this question. The Greek text of the passage rendered by Westcott and Hort shows a beautiful and elaborate design of amazing numerical features. If even one letter is changed to another, the entire numeric scheme fails. But the Greek text of the passage from which the Revised Version is translated shows no numeric design. The newly discovered facts thus prove that Westcott and Hort give the correct reading of the passage.

WHAT IS THE LAST WORD OF THE BIBLE?

The Authorized or King James Version follows certain Greek manuscripts and gives the word "Amen" as the last word in the Bible. The Revised Version likewise concludes the Bible with this word. The Revisers do not even intimate that some authorities omit the word. Westcott and Hort in their Greek New

Testament follow other Greek manuscripts and con-
clude the Testament with the word "saints." Tischendorff, Alford, and other editors differ.

The amazing design of numeric features or facts
discovered in the structure of the Greek text used
by Westcott and Hort definitely settle the question
concerning the correct reading of the last verse in the
Bible. The numerical facts prove that they are right
in ending the New Testament with the word "saints."

THE TRUE READING OF BIBLE PASSAGES IS DETERMINED WITH REMARKABLE PRECISION AND ACCURACY

Readers will be amazed to learn that the perfect
numeric designs which underlie the very structure of
the original Bible text make it possible to detect any
letter or word that may have been **added, omitted,** or
transposed through the error of a copyist. The extraordinary mathematical designs in a profound manner
determine the exact order of words, spelling, etc. Every question concerning the true reading of a passage
—every single disputed matter, even to the slightest
variation of text between manuscripts—is conclusively
settled by the elaborate design of numerical features.

Just as an astronomer, who knows definite astro-
nomical calculations and the position of various planets,
can determine where and when certain other planets
will appear, so one who knows definite numerical calculations of the Bible and the position of various letters,
words, or books, can immediately determine where
certain other letters, words, or books should occur.

Place Values And Order Numbers

The proper order of Bible words is determined by the numeric designs in the "place values" and "order numbers" of the words. It must be remembered that the "numeric values" of words are not affected or changed by their order in the text. Regardless of the order of the words the numeric values remain the same. Therefore the proper order of the words cannot be determined merely by the designs in the numeric values. The separate numeric designs, however, in the place values and 'order numbers furnish methods of determining the correct order of words.

For example, various manuscripts differ as to the order of the names of our Lord. Some manuscript copies give the order as "Jesus Christ" in certain passages, while other copies in the same particular passages give the order as "Christ Jesus." Which is correct? The proper order for each particular passage is definitely established by the numeric designs in the place values and order numbers of the words. The amazing numeric designs always give a definite and clear answer—the true order shows numeric designs and the false order does not. A change in order invariably destroys perfect designs in the place values and order numbers.

The correct spelling of words is determined by the designs in the order numbers. For example in a certain passage in some manuscripts the following words are spelled "Mariam" and "Daveid." In the same passage in other manuscripts the words are spelled "Mary" and "David." Which is the correct spelling?

The elaborate numeric designs in the place values conclusively prove that "Mary" and "David" are the proper spellings of the words. It is also possible to determine whether a certain number of letters should form one large word or two smaller words.

Since there is no punctuation in the ancient manuscripts, it is sometimes difficult to determine whether certain sentences are intended to be in the form of commands or questions. Numeric designs in the place values even settle issues of this nature. They definitely settle the dispute as to the correct "interpretation" of any passage, and even long debated questions concerning the true authorship of certain books of the Bible. For example, numeric designs unquestionably prove that the Apostle Paul was the writer of the Epistle to the Hebrews.

It is remarkable also to note that a profound "cross-section" method—a system of multiplication—makes it possible to promptly detect and check on any errors which may have been made when determining the place and order of words in the vocabulary.

It is indeed marvelous to think of the many separate systems of designs which run through each letter and word. Not only is there a definite numeric scheme in the "numeric values" of each letter and word, but there are also separate designs in the place values, values, and order numbers, of each letter and word. Each pattern or design serves its own particular purpose. In addition to these separate systems of designs there is the amazing "cross section" check on the vocabulary, and there are the many other numeric features and designs which permeate the text in every conceivable manner. It is marvelous indeed! All these systems together conclusively settle any question concerning the true reading of a passage.

One separate scheme or numeric design is convincing enough to demonstrate the divine inspiration of any passage, but when all these many separate systems of designs which run through each letter and word of a passage are combined, the argument is ˙ simply unshakeable. Every letter and word is so intricately intertwined and interlocked by these different systems of designs that it is simply impossible to move a letter or word either to the right or to the left without destroying the perfect patterns. The very order˙ of every letter and word is definitely designed. Each letter and word has its own special place. Such perfect order—such complex systems of designs with their astonishing precision and accuracy, indeed could not have occurred accidentally. As an illustration, suppose that the sixty or sixty-five pieces of an alarm clock were placed in a box. One could shake that box year in and year out and those pieces would never go in their proper places accidentally. The perfect order and the complex numeric systems of the Bible cannot be attributed to chance, or even to human design—they can only be divine.

The Bible itself claims that divine inspiration extends not only to every sentence and every word, but even to the smallest letter and the smallest mark. In Matthew 5:17, 18, when Jesus said that not one "jot" or one "tittle" would pass from the law till all be fulfilled, He referred to the smallest letter (jot) and the smallest mark or point (tittle), thus indicating that even they were inspired.

The numerical facts demonstrate that the words, syllables, letters, and even every jot and tittle are numbered and have their own special, divinely appointed place in the text. God controlled the writers and placed every jot and tittle just where He wanted it. He controlled the spelling of every word and the number of its occurrences in the various Bible books. The Bible is scientifically proved to be divinely inspired, not in a loose or general way—not only in "thought," but in actual word and letter. The Great Designer precisely planned the exact order of every word and letter, and every jot and tittle. Christ's significant statement, "The Scripture cannot be broken" is proved to be true.

Numerical designs definitely settle the true reading of every Bible passage where the various manuscript copies differ slightly in the order of words, spelling, etc. The exact text which was originally written by the Bible writers long ago has been reproduced and ascertained with absolute certainty. Every word, syllable, letter, and mark of God's Word has been restored to its original perfection and purity. The exact wording of every disputed passage is definitely settled by the mathematical designs, and by them alone—by designs which are strangely concealed beneath the very surface of the Bible text. Indeed God has protected and preserved His Word in a wonderful manner. It has come down to us with amazing perfection and purity—without a tinge or speck of corruption within or without.

When one considers the similarity of various letters and the difficulty of copying large manuscripts by hand, he will agree that the manuscript copies, irrespective of their slight variations, have been transmitted to us with marvelous accuracy.

In the Hebrew there are certain letters which appear very much alike. For example, the first letter in the Hebrew alphabet denotes one, and with two little points above it, it denotes a thousand. The twenty-second or last letter of the Hebrew alphabet denotes four hundred, but the fifth letter, which looks very much like it and could be easily mistaken for it, denotes five. A very slight error of the copyist would therefore make an utter change in meaning. The followng letters could be easily confounded:

ת — ה   400 and   5

ח — ה   8 and   5

ב — כ   2 and   20

ג — נ   3 and   50

ד — ר   4 and   200

In Deuteronomy 6:4, if the Hebrew letter which has a value of 4 were changed to the very similar letter which has a numeric value of 200, the verse would read "the Lord our God is a false Lord," instead of "the Lord our God is one Lord." A change in these same letters in Exodus 34:14 would make that passage read, "Thou shalt not worship the one true God."

Since each letter stands for a number, it is clear that a change in even a single letter changes the numeric value of the entire passage. The omission of or a change in a single letter, to say nothing of a whole word, at once destroys many features of a perfect numeric design. In fact the design as a whole is destroyed by the addition of one word. In one case all is harmony, and the elaborate scheme of sevens is seen at once, while in the other case, all is confusion if something foreign is introduced into the delicate numerical system mysteriously recorded in the Bible by the Holy Spirit.

The following is a striking illustration of the remarkable precision and accuracy made possible by the presence of the numerical facts in the very structure of the Bible text.

A certain Bible concordance prepared by C. F. Hudson, supervised by H. L. Hastings, and checked by Ezra Abbot, lists what were evidently thought to be all of the Bible references in which the word "Moses" occurs. According to the concordance the name appears in exactly 846 Bible references. This number of course is out of harmony with various numeric designs which run through the Bible. According to certain numeric designs the name would be expected to occur a number of times which divides perfectly by seven. Of course 846 does not divide evenly by seven, but 847 does—it is 121 sevens. What is the trouble? Was one of the references omitted from the concordance?

Yes, a reference to Moses which that certain edition of the concordance does not list is found in the book of Hebrews. The scholarly gentlemen who prepared this concordance apparently overlooked this verse, but the error is detected by the designs of numerical facts which occur in the very structure of the Bible text.

It has been stated that the newly discovered facts definitely settle various important questions in regard to the Bible. Three of these questions have already been discussed. They are restated below and are included with an additional three.

SIX SUPREMELY IMPORTANT QUESTIONS NOW DEFINITELY SETTLED BY THE NEWLY DISCOVERED FACTS

(1)   It has been scientifically demonstrated in preceding chapters that the amazing numerical facts definitely settle the question whether the Bible is actually a God inspired book as it claims or whether it is a mere human production. It was shown that the amazing numerical structure of the Bible could not possibly have occurred accidentally but that it was designed, and the phenomenal design could not possibly have been planned and carried out by man, but is the work of God Himself. (Chapters 1-5)

(2)   The newly discovered facts definitely settle the question whether certain passages are genuine God inspired passages or whether they are mere human interpolations or additions to the inspired Bible. The disputes over passages such as Mark 16:9-20, John 7:53 to 8:11, are now forever settled. (Chapter 6)

(3)   The amazing numerical facts also definitely settle the question concerning the true reading of passages.   The slightest variation of text between manuscript copies is detected by the design of numerical facts, and thus the correct reading is easily determined.   The numerical facts not only make the Bible sure regarding its supernatural divine inspiration, but they settle the text and its meaning, such as Isaiah 9:5, I Cor. 13:3.   They settle all disputes concerning matters of spelling, punctuation, order of letters, words, etc. (Chapter 7)

(4)   The newly discovered numerical facts definitely settle the question regarding the correct number of books the Bible should contain.   The Roman and Greek Catholic Churches include in the Old Testament of their Bibles, 14 books known as the Apocrypha, which Protestants do not include.   The books of the Apocrypha date from 300 B. C. to 100 A. D.   With the exception of these books, the Roman and Greek Catholic Bibles are practically identical with the Protestant Bible.   What is the correct number of Bible books?

There are many marvelous numeric designs which run through all of the 66 books of the Protestant Bible as a whole—patterns which bind these books into one great unit.   If a single book is added or removed, certain elaborate numeric designs or chains which tie these books together are completely destroyed.   Furthermore, there is no evidence of numerical features and designs in the very text of the Apocrypha.   Thus the Bibles of the Roman and Greek Catholic Church, so far as the number of books is concerned, is proved to be incorrect. The numerical facts thus act as an automatic check against tampering with the divinely planned number of books.

(5) The newly discovered facts also definitely settle the question concerning the correct order of the Bible books. The books of the English Bible are arranged in different order from that in which they are found in the Hebrew Received Text and the Greek Text. The order of the books as given in the original Hebrew and Greek is not accidental but divinely designed. A phenomenal numeric design runs through the order numbers of the books in such a peculiar and marvelous manner that if the books are taken out of their proper order the particular numeric scheme fails. The numeric facts thus act as an automatic check against tampering with the divinely designed order of the 66 Bible books. This is a large and marvelous subject.

(6) The amazing newly discovered facts even settle the long disputed question concerning the correct Chronology of the Bible. The exact dates of Bible events from the time of Adam are determined and definitely established, and are arranged in their proper sequence by the profound numeric designs in the structure of the text. The designs furnish data for an exact system of chronology in which the outstanding dates of Bible history divide perfectly by seven. This also is a great subject in itself. Volumes could be devoted to the relation of the numeric facts to Bible Chronology. The subject is so vast and comprehensive that no attempt is made to discuss it in this publication.

The writer, naturally, has not attempted to give a full or detailed account of the science of Bible Numerics, but has merely endeavored to present a systematic account of the nature and scope of this newly discovered science. Many departments and phases of it, such as, place values, values, order numbers, higher numerics, number of books, order of books, chronology, and other comprehensive systems of designs, have been barely mentioned. Nevertheless, the reader may grasp the general idea.

The amazing numeric facts and designs in the structure of the original Bible text are indelible. They are impressed upon and interwoven in the text in such a peculiar and marvelous manner that no power on earth can blot them out. They are woven into God's Word as a thread is woven in a dollar bill to assure its genuineness. They are imprinted on the pages of Scripture as watermarks are imprinted in paper for verification and identification. They guard the Bible against errors and interpolations as the intricate designs on a bank note or check guard against counterfeits and interpolations. Indeed, God has stamped or marked His Word in a marvelous manner!

The many profound numeric designs in the structure of the Bible text are not only beyond the attainment of the Bible writers themselves, but no doubt the writers did not even know of the formation and presence of these elaborate patterns in the text. No doubt these men were so completely controlled by God's power and wisdom in writing His exact words that they were wholly unaware of the fact that every letter and word was being arranged according to a definite mathematical plan. No doubt the writers were unconscious of the fact that the Spirit was introducing, weaving, and mysteriously concealing beautiful patterns and intricately intertwined designs in the very structure of their writings. Even the Bible passages themselves appear to be wholly innocent of the slightest attempt at design—they read beautifully and naturally.

It has been demonstrated that the vast numerical structure of the Bible is a supernatural divine work. While it is utterly impossible for human beings to construct a book on such a marvelous mathematical design, it is only the **normal work** of God, the great Creator, Who has carefully placed—

NUMBERS IN ALL OF NATURE

The number system of God is stamped upon all His works. All departments of nature are based on a system of mathematics—great mathematical laws govern the activities of the entire universe.

For instance, in the sphere of light, there are exactly seven colors. The seven colors merged together form light. In the sphere of music there are exactly seven whole tones in the scale, while every eighth note begins a new octave and is merely a repetition of the first note. The seven colors correspond to the seven notes in music, and sounds that harmonize correspond with colors that harmonize, while discords in color correspond with discords in music.

The human body is completely renewed or changed every seven years. Every part of the body is constantly throwing off old effete matter, and constantly receiving deposits of new and living matter. In seven years the whole structure is altered down to the minutest particles and becomes essentially a new body. In certain diseases, the seventh, fourteenth, and twenty-first are the critical days. Man's pulse beats slower every seventh day whether he is sick or well. In diseases resulting from physical exhaustion, the pulse changes every seventh day. With the human being the period of gestation is 280 days (7x40). Indeed, seven is stamped upon physiology. Is it not significant that God ordained every seventh day to be a day of rest, and that He declared man's years to be "Three-score and ten." (7x10)?

With animals, the period of gestation of the mouse is 21 (7x3) days. The hare and rat 28 (7x4) days. The cat 56 (7x8) days. The dog 63 (7x9) days. The lion 98 (7x14) days. The sheep 147 (7x21) days. With birds, the incubation of the common hen is 21 (7x3) days. The duck 28 (7x4) days.

God's mathematical laws are at work in all departments of nature. Sometimes one certain number is the dominant factor, then again another is the basic number.

The Creator's law of design for the snow flakes is the number six. All snowflakes are different, yet they are all alike with either six points or six sides.

The number eleven as well as seven is stamped on music. The number of vibrations in a second for each note is a multiple of eleven, and the difference in the number of vibrations between each note is also a multiple of eleven. For example, the difference between Do and Re is 33, between Fa and Sol 44, always a multiple of eleven.

The Science of Botany reveals that the different sections of flowers are arranged according to particular numbers and their multiples. For example the basic number of the buttercup is five. There are 5 sepals in the calyx, 5 petals in the corolla, 5 carpels in the pistil, 15, 20, 25, or some other number which is exactly so many fives of stamens in the androecium. Similarly, the basic number of the daffodil is 3, that of the mignonette 4, the wild rose 5. etc. Thus God stamps His creation with a mathematical pattern.

In Chemistry no two substances can unite without observing definite mathematical proportions. The planets of the heavens are governed according to mathematical laws. Indeed, nature does not operate by chance, but by design. God's number system is found throughout the universe much more extensively than is commonly supposed. Volumes could be devoted to showing design in nature. God is the Great Numberer and Mathematician of all creation. Every department of nature bears His mathematical signature.

"He made the stars . . . And God set them in
the firmament of the heaven."   Gen. 1:16-17

"He counteth the number of the stars" Ps. 147:4 R. V.

He "bringeth out their host by number"   Isa. 40:26

God "hath **measured** the waters in the hollow
of His hand, and **meted** out the heaven
with a **span**, and comprehended the dust
of the earth in a **measure**, and **weighed** the
mountains in **scales**, and the hills in a
balance."   Isaiah 40:12

If God **placed** the stars in their proper order, and
numbered them and **measured** the waters and **weighed**
the mountains, is it surprising or incredible that He has
placed the words and letters of His book in **exact**
order, and **numbered** them, and guided them into com-
binations of numbers?

The same God Who created the universe and was
careful to weave designs and intricate patterns into the
smallest detail of creation, has taken the same care
with His Word. He has placed the same peculiarity
in both.

"The very hairs of your head are all **numbered**"
(counted) Matthew 10:30.

The word "numbered" in Greek is "arithmeo"
the very word from which our English word "Arithmetic" is derived. If God counts the very hairs of
our heads, is it strange that He has counted the words
and letters of His Scripture?

CHAPTER EIGHT

Who Discovered The Facts? How And When Were They Discovered? Why Were They Not Discovered Until Recently?

The discovery of thousands of numerical facts beneath the very surface of the original Bible text has been the lifetime task of a single individual—Dr. Ivan Panin,* a famous Russian Scientist.

Among the thousands who have read the Hebrew and Greek text of the Bible, Ivan Panin was the very first to discover the amazing numerical facts which lie beneath the surface of the Scripture—the facts which scientifically prove that the Bible could not possibly have been written by mere human beings alone, but that it is a supernatural, God inspired, God given book

Today, after more than a half century of diligent and tedious labor on his phenomenal numerical discoveries, Mr. Panin, in his eighty-sixth year, presents an array of facts which astound the world. The original manuscripts of his work consist of approximately 40,000 pages. Upon these pages, many of

*Ivan Panin died at Aldershot, Ontario, Canada, on October 30, 1942, shortly after this book was first published.

which are now yellow with age, Mr. Panin has carefully and thoughtfully written millions of figures. The completion of his work has required persistent labor from 12 to 18 hours daily throughout the past fifty years.

Mr. Panin is of the same caliber as the famous Simon Newcomb and is without doubt the greatest mathematical genius since Newcomb's time. In discovering these thousands of numerical facts Mr. Panin has fulfilled a ministry and has accomplished a life work utterly different from that of any other human being who has ever lived. Indeed he has a place among the greatest and most famous men in the history of the world.

An individual whose life-work has been so outstanding as Mr. Panin's deserves an entire book devoted to his biography. However here in a few pages the writer has attempted to present some of the more important facts concerning this distinguished person and his work.

Mr. Panin was born in Russia, December 12, 1855. As a young man he was an active Nihilist and participated in plots against the Czar and his government. At an early age he was exiled from Russia. After spending a number of years in Germany furthering his education, he came to the United States. Soon after his arrival, Mr. Panin entered Harvard University. He was a personal friend of the famous Professor William James, and President Eliot of Harvard.

Mr. Panin is a brilliant scholar and a Master of Literary Criticism. After his college days he became an outstanding lecturer on the subject of literary criticism. He lectured on Carlyle, Emerson, Tolstoy, and on Russian literature, etc., being paid as high 'as $200.00 for each address. His lectures were delivered in colleges and before exclusive literary clubs in many cities of the United States and Canada. During this time Mr. Panin became well known as a firm agnostic— so well known that when he discarded his agnosticism, and accepted the Christian faith the newspapers carried headlines telling of his conversion. Professor James, who was reputed to be the greatest Metaphysician of his time, remarked, "What a pity that Mr. Panin is cracked on religion. A great philosopher was spoiled in him." Prior to his conversion Mr. Panin wrote some three thousand aphorisms and many remarkable essays, which are indeed a memorial to his days as a Master of Literary Criticism. Mr. Panin was also an editor of two daily newspapers. He is a gifted writer and a brilliant and eloquent speaker.

HOW AND WHEN DID MR. PANIN DISCOVER THE FIRST OF THESE NUMERICAL FACTS?

It has already been stated that Mr. Panin has devoted more than a half century to the discovery of these amazing numerical facts. To be exact, it was in the year 1890 that Mr. Panin made the discovery that a phenomenal mathematical structure underlay the text and vocabulary of the Greek New Testament.

Mr. Panin was casually reading the first verse of the Gospel of John in the Greek—"In the beginning was the Word, and the Word was with (the) God, and the Word was God." The question came to his mind, "Why does the Greek word for 'the' precede the word 'God' in one case, but not in the other?"

Therefore in one column he made a list of all the New Testament passages in which the word "God" occurs with the article "the," and in another column he made a list of all the passages in which the word "God" occurs without the article. On comparing the two sums he was struck with the numeric relation between them. He then followed the same procedure on the word "Christ" and on other words, and found amazing numeric facts. This was the beginning of the profound numerical discoveries which are now called the Science of Bible Numerics. Mr. Panin has used the Greek text of Westcott and Hort as a basis for most of his work. However, he has not wholly confined himself to that text.

Since discovering the first features in 1890 Mr. Panin has earnestly devoted his entire life to one definite and specific purpose. For the past half century he has toiled faithfully and tirelessly with undaunted perseverance. He has devoted himself so persistently to counting letters and words, figuring numeric values, making concordances, and working out mathematical problems, that on several occasions his health completely failed. Regardless of the tremendous mental and physical strain he has labored faithfully and diligently for the past fifty years.

Mr. Panin has permitted nothing to hinder him from fulfilling his life work. At one time he was offered a very tempting position as president of a college. However, he rejected the offer. He chose rather to devote his life to discovering numerical facts and demonstrating the divine inspiration of the Bible. Since 1890 Mr. Panin has trusted God to provide for him. Some think it strange he should have discontinued his seemingly profitable lecture work as a Master of Literary Criticism at $200.00 a night, for the purpose of counting Bible numbers, letters, syllables, words, etc.

This distinguished person is a man of extraordinary resources in scholarship. He is keen-minded and alert and possesses amazing analytical and dissecting ability. He is eminently open and scientific. He assumes nothing, but bases all on observed facts— facts of a positive, irrefutable, unparalleled sort. He pursues his way with calmness and is positive of the ground he covers. He is a complete master of himself and of the facts at his command.

Mr. Panin is an ardent and devout Christian—a "born again" child of God. His pleasing personality radiates the abiding presence of the Christ within. This refined gentleman and his lovely wife live quiet, humble lives on a small Canadian farm, far removed from the busy city activities. Mr. Panin is very modest and conservative. He prefers to be called Mr. Panin rather than Dr. Panin, and is reluctant about publicizing facts concerning his own life story. He points out that the Apostles left little or no life stories of themselves, but **exalted Christ instead.** Incidentally Mr. **Panin is a citizen of the United States.**

THE EXTENT OF MR. PANIN'S OUTSTANDING LIFE WORK

It was necessary for Mr. Panin to prepare and construct special "tools" before he could begin the actual work of discovering the thousands of numerical facts in the structure of the Bible. He has had to construct concordances, vocabularies and other analyses of the Bible which require the utmost accuracy to the slightest detail.

His specially prepared concordance of the Greek New Testament words consists of a thousand pages and contains every one of the 137,903 occurrences of the New Testament Greek words. The words are arranged in alphabetical order and all the references of the chapters and verses are neatly listed directly under each word. Of course certain words occur hundreds of times throughout the New Testament, yet each occurrence is listed in the concordance. The best Greek concordances in print were not complete enough or accurate enough for Mr. Panin's work, therefore it was necessary for him to construct a concordance of his own.

Mr. Panin's specially prepared concordance for the forms of the New Testament Greek words is a manuscript which contains more than 2,000 pages. It is constructed on the same plan as the first concordance, and contains about twice as much material.

The construction of these two manuscripts, needless to say, was no small task. More than six years of tedious and continuous labor were required to complete them. But this is not all—Mr. Panin has prepared special books for the vocabulary words of the Greek New Testament. It is strictly a scientific vocabulary. Each New Testament word is listed and there are sixteen columns of numeric data for each word. Four columns containing the order number, place value, numeric value, value, precede each word. Behind each word there are twelve columns containing the number of occurrences, number of forms, syllables, letters, writers, books, diphthongs, etc. The completion of the vocabulary required more than two years of strenuous labor. In some of his work Mr. Panin has marked certain words in green, red, blue, and purple ink. Each color bears some particular significance.

All this work was merely the preparation of some "tools" which were necessary before Mr. Panin could begin the actual work of discovering countless thousands of numerical facts. Since the work was begun, Mr. Panin has accumulated some 40,000 pages of material on which he has made calculations, worked out mathematical problems, and recorded numerical facts. Upon these pages he has thoughtfully and prayerfully written millions of small and neat appearing figures. His work constitutes volumes and his discoveries are seemingly without end. Throughout the past fifty years Mr. Panin has been earnestly devoting from twelve to eighteen hours daily exploring the vast numerical structure of the Bible. The mental and physical toil involved has been tremendous.

It is noteworthy that Mr. Panin has not done his work for "pay" neither has he "paid" anyone to assist him. During these years he has needed a capable secretary and persons to assist him in other departments of his enterprise. However he has felt that this type of work could not be truly done for a "salary." He has needed volunteers—persons with a God-given devotion to the work—dozens of vigorous, resourceful young men with enthusiasm for the cause, not persons who require salaries. For many years when Mr. Panin first began his work he hoped and prayed for even a small number of persons who would stand by him and assist him in his God given work, but it seems many had no time, others were not interested, etc., so he had to go on alone. For many years he toiled, sometimes cheerlessly and sadly, but his labor was not in vain. Finally he triumphed over every obstacle and hardship. After more than a half century of continuous labor and undaunted perseverance he was able to see the task completed, and today as a result of his faithfulness and courage, he presents an array of facts which astound the world.

The fact that Mr. Panin has been able to accomplish this immense task single handed is indeed a testimony to his diligence. The writer knows of no other example of perseverance and diligence anywhere in history which equals or even compares to the fifty years continuous labor of this one man. Indeed Mr. Panin is an intellectual giant and a prodigious worker.

Mr. Panin's specially prepared concordances, vocabularies, and many of the pages of other numeric data are now turning yellow with age.

A page from the specially prepared concordance of Greek New Testament words. The book consists of one thousand such pages. (actual size)

√ δε (2)

Jas 1: 4.5.6.9.10.13.14.15, 19.22.25
2: 2.3.6.9.10,11,11,14,15, 16.20.23.25
3: 3.8.14.17.18
4: 6.6.7.11.12.16
5: 12.12   - 37

1 Pet. 1: 7.8.12,21,25,25-
2: 4.7.9.10,10,14.23
3: 8.9.11.12.14,15,18
4: 6.7.16,16.17,18
5: 5.5.10   29

2 Pet. 1: 5.5.6.6.6,7.7.13.15
2: 1.9.10.12.16.20
3: 7.8.10.10,13.18 -...

1 John 1: 3.7
2: 2.5,11.17
3: 12.11
4: 18
5: 5.20   - 11

3 John 12.14   - 2

Jude 1.5.8.8.9.10,10.14 17.20.23.24, - 1/2

Rom. 1: 8/12.13,17 - 1·8
2: 2.3.5.8.8,10/7.25
3: 4.4.5,7.19.21.22
4: 2.4.5.5.15.20.23
5: 3.4.5.5.8.11.13.16, 20.20   -3ε
6: 8.10.11.17.17.18 12, 22.22.23   -10
7: 2.3.6.8.9.9.9.14.16 17.18.20.23.25.25

√ δε (2)   185

Rom. 8: 5.6.8.9.9.10.10.11.13.17.17.23.24 25.26.27.28.30.30.34 -35
9: 6.10.13.18.21.22.27.30.31
10: 6.10.14.14.15.17.20.21 -17
11: 6.7.8.12.13.16.17.17.18.20, 22.23.28.30   - 14
12: 5.5.6
13: 1.2.3.4.12.12
14: 1.2.3.4.5.10.23.23 -1
15: 1.5.9.13.14.15.20.23.23.25 29.30.33   - 13
16: 1.17.19.19.20.25.26 - 7

1 Cor 1: 10.10.12.12.12.16.18.12.23 23.24.20   -12
2: 6.6(10).12.14.15.15.16
3: 4.5.6.8.10.11.12.15.15.23.23
4: 3.4.6.7.7.10.10.10.19
5: 3.11.12
6: 13.13.14.17.18   ε
7: 1.2.3.4.6.7.7.8.9.10.11.12 14.15.15.25.25.28.28.28 29.32.33.34.35.36.37.37 39.40   -30
8: 1.2.3.7.8.12.9
9: 15.15.18.23.24.25.25
10: 4.6.11.11.13.20.28.29
11: 2.3.3.3, 5.6.7.12.15.16 17.21.28.31.32.34 -38
12: 1.4.4.7.8.9.10.10.10.10.11, 12.18.19.20.20.21.24.27.31
13: 1.2.3.6.8.10.12.12.13.13-...
14: 1.1.2.3.4.5.5.5.6.14.15.15, 20.22.23.24.24.28.28.29 30.35.39.40 -...

A page from the specially prepared concordance for the forms of the Greek New Testament words. The manuscript consists of two thousand such pages.
(actual size)

A page from the specially prepared book of Greek New Testament Vocabulary words. The book consists of 221 pages. (reduced half size)

	Place	Numerics	Value		Greek	Strong	Syll.	Letters	Writers	Books	Apostrophe		Gospel	Acts- Epist.	Cath. Paul	Revelation
3505	101	858	959	οστοχγς	2	1	4	7	2	2			1		4	
3506	52	318	370	οσμη	6	3	2	4					1		4	
3507	66	540	606	οσος	109	7	2	4					1	2	3 4	5
3508	85	695	780	οστιον	4	3	3	6					1		4	
3509	79	780	859	στις	126	7	2	5					1	2	3 4	5
3510	135	1021	1156	οστεακινος	2	2		10	2	2			1		4	
3511	123	1288	1411	οσφεγοις	1	1	3	8	1	1			1		4	
3512	92	1370	1462	οσφυς	8	5	2	5					1	2	3 4	
3513	48	721	769	οται	122	1	2	4					1	2	3 4	5
3514	39	375	414	οτι	101	1	2	8					1	2	3 4	5
3515	43	380	423	οτι	1317	1	2	3					1	2	3 4	5
3516	35	770	505	ου	1619	3	1	2	8	26	1		1	2	3 4	5
3517	26	471	497	ουα	1	1	2	3	1	1	1		1			
3518	75	781	526	ουαι	46	1	2	4	6	6	2				3	5
3519	94	1015	609	ουδαμως	1	1	3	7	1	1	1		1			
3520	44	479	523	ουδε	141	2	2	4		1			1	2	3 4	5
3521	71	689	760	ουδεις	217	5	2	5		2			1	2	3 4	5
3522	66	530	596	ουδεμια	11	2	4	7		1			1	2	3 4	
3523	99	934	1033	ουδεποτε	16	1	4	8		1			1	2	4	
3524	84	1359	1443	ουδεπω	3	1	3	6		1			1	2		
3525	75	694	769	ουθεις	7	2	2	6		2			1	2	4	
3526	78	805	883	ουκετι	47	1	3	6		1			1	2	4	5
3527	93	1010	1103	ουκουν	1	1	2	6		2			1			
3528	48	520	568	ουν	494	1	1	3		1			1	2	3 4	5

One of the approximately 40,000 work sheets.
(reduced half size)

The preceding pages have given us a glimpse of Mr. Panin's extensive life work. Words fail to adequately describe this comprehensive accomplishment. To say that it is extraordinary indeed is not sufficient!

Two outstanding results of Mr. Panin's lifetime labor are his—

NUMERIC GREEK NEW TESTAMENT
and
NUMERIC ENGLISH NEW TESTAMENT

Both volumes are commendable and scholarly pieces of work. The "Numeric Greek New Testament" is a complete Greek Testament without any alternative readings. The text was established by means of the newly discovered numeric designs which pervade the Scripture. Mr. Panin has settled every one of the alternative readings left by Wescott and Hort in their Greek text of the New Testament. He presents a pure and accurate Greek text—an indisputable text which is exactly the same as that of the original manuscripts which holy men of old wrote by the inspiration of God. It is the first Greek New Testament published which has its text based upon the newly discovered numerical structure of the Bible—a remarkable piece of work indeed! It is a volume of 514 pages, printed at the Oxford University Press.

The "Numeric English New Testament" is Mr. Panin's translation of his Greek New Testament. The chief aim of his English translation, next to that of furnishing a pure text, is to place the reader, as far as possible, on the same footing with the Greek. It is indeed a superb piece of English, yet it follows the Greek text very closely and gives as literal a rendering of the original as possible. Mr. Panin's many years of study and careful examination of every jot and tittle of the original Bible text, and his ability as an outstanding literary man, make him a fit and well equipped editor. His New Testament is unquestionably the finest and most accurate translation into English. It is one of the latest translations published, and is the only one which has its text based upon the newly discovered numerical structure of the Scripture. Students of the Bible are not doing their work justice unless they study this splendid edition. It is truly a beautiful translation, a volume of 610 pages in clear and readable type, printed at the Oxford University Press and published by The Book Society of Canada.

Some have thoughtlessly attempted to verify Mr. Panin's work by counting letters and words in their English King James translation or in some other translation of the Bible. The same features which Mr. Panin has discovered in the Hebrew and Greek text of the Bible could not be expected to be found in translations of that text. This is easily understood. For example, the Greek sentence "Edakrusen 'o Iesous" is a sentence of three Greek words, but translated into English it is a sentence of only two words—"Jesus wept." There are sixteen letters in the Greek sentence but only nine letters in the English translation of it. There are six letters in the Greek word 'Ιησοῦς but only five letters in its English translation—"Jesus." Furthermore, the letters of the English alphabet do not have numeric values as the Hebrew and Greek letters have. Also words of one language are not simply transliterated in other languages. An example is the word "Venice." This is the English spelling. But the French is "Venise;" the German is "Venedig;" while the Italian is "Venezia."

The numeric features which Mr. Panin has discovered are not based on the letters and words of any English translation or any other translation of the Bible. They are based entirely on the letters and words of the Hebrew and Greek in which the Bible was originally written. Thus it is easily understood that it is difficult for many readers to verify a great number of Mr. Panin's statements.

For the benefit of scholarly readers Mr. Panin has printed special monographs in which he has given the Greek texts of numerous Bible passages. In the monographs he has included the vocabularies and many other details of original numeric data which pertain to the various texts. These charts and tables of calculations were made available so no one could say it was impossible to check Mr Panin's findings. The original numeric data has enabled any scholar to easily verify for himself every statement Mr. Panin has made in the monographs. Throughout the years, Mr. Panin has sent these printed copies of numeric data to scholars whom the material especially concerns. To the best of his ability he has seen to it that none remain in ignorance of his discoveries.

At one time, a number of years ago, Mr. Panin sent some of his numeric material with vocabularies

and other details to nine rationalists, whom he respect-
fully and publicly invited to refute him. He challenged
Dr. Charles W. Eliot, President of Harvard University;
Professor J. Henry Thayer, also of Harvard; Dr. W. R.
Harper, President of the University of Chicago; Dr.
Minot J. Savage, and others, saying in print, "Gentle-
men, will you kindly refute my facts; will you refute
the conclusions?"

Mr. Panin received several replies. One was not
"interested" in his "arithmetical" facts, two "regret-
ted" that they "had no time" to give heed thereto.
Another "did not mean to be unkind, but . . ." The
others were silent.

A number of years ago some of Mr. Panin's
numeric material appeared in a Sunday edition of the
"New York Sun." The following is a quotation:

"Now there are three ways, but three ways only,
in which to refute my argument:

"(1) By showing that it is possible for two books
to be written each after the other; that it is possible
for eight men (the eight New Testament Writers) to
write in turn each after the other seven; that it is
possible for 27 books (of the New Testament) to be
written each in its turn last; that it is possible for
some 537 pages (of the Westcott and Hort Greek New
Testament Text) to be written each in its turn last!
(Chapter 5, number 3.)

"(2) My argument can also be refuted by showing that the facts I present are not facts; that the
Greek Alpha does not stand for one, Beta for two,

Gamma for three, and so on; that the additions I make are not additions; in short, that the numerics I presented to the readers of the Sun are delusions, figments, fabrications, frauds—miserable cheats, in short.

"(3) Lastly, my argument can also be refuted by showing that even though my facts be true, my arithmetic faultless, and my collocation of numerics honest, that men could have written thus without inspiration from above.

"No sane man will try to refute me by the first method. To refute me by the second method I herewith respectfully invite any or all of the following to prove that my facts are not facts: namely Messrs. Lyman Abbott, Washington Gladden, Herber Newton, Minot J. Savage, Presidents Eliot of Harvard, White of Cornell, and Harper of the University of Chicago, Professor J. Henry Thayer of Harvard, and and Dr. Briggs, and any other prominent higher critic so called. They may associate with themselves, if they choose, all the contributors to the ninth edition of the Encyclopedia Britannica who wrote its articles on Biblical subjects, together with a dozen mathematicians of the calibre of Professor Simon Newcomb. The heavier the calibre of either scholar or mathematician, the more satisfactory to me.

"They will find that my facts are facts. And since they are facts, I am ready to take them to any three prominent lawyers, or, better still, to any judge of the superior or supreme court, and abide by his decision as to whether the conclusion is not necessary that Inspiration alone can account for the facts, if they are facts.

"All I should ask would be that the judge treat the case as he would any other case that comes before him: declining to admit matters for discussion as irrelevant when they are irrelevant; and listening patiently to both sides, as he does in any trial."

No attempt has been made to deal with Mr. Panin's undeniable facts or with the unavoidable conclusion. A destructive critic can do nothing in the way of refuting these facts—all he can do is ignore them. Are Mr. Panin's figures wrong? If so, where are they wrong? If they are not, then the inferences are indisputable. One cannot argue with mathematics.

WHY WERE THE NUMERICAL FACTS NOT DISCOVERED UNTIL RECENTLY?

There seems to be a reason why the thousands of mysteriously hidden numeric facts remained concealed for so many centuries before they were finally revealed. The discovery of these facts was no doubt withheld until this very day and age, because the Holy Spirit of God, Who caused these features to be so arranged in the structure of the Bible, foresaw that the greatest attacks ever waged against the Bible would occur in the age in which we live.

The fiercest attacks ever made against the Bible were begun a number of years ago when the forces of modernism and destructive higher criticism began their cunning internal attacks. Never before in the history of the church has the Bible been torn to pieces by those who profess to be ministers and teachers and lovers of it. Previous to these latter days, only atheists and skeptics boldly denounced and ridiculed the

Bible, but recently modernists who stand behind sacred pulpits denounce and ridicule the very book they are being well paid to teach. Today so called "Christians" are attacking the Bible, whereas it ought to be defended by everyone who calls himself a Christian. If people were as inconsistent as that in business, they would be dismissed from their positions immediately. Higher critics and so called scientific thinkers in supposed "Christian" colleges and seminaries disgracefully attempt to reduce the Bible to nothing more than a collection of human writings which are filled with inaccuracies and contradictions and the vagaries of the human imagination. This attack against the Bible has come from within the Church itself, and as a result many mere "church members" have been deceived into substituting modernism for godly old-fashioned funda-mentalism. The present Bible-attack is against the entire foundation of the Christian faith—the divine inspiration of the Scriptures—and is indeed the most cunning and severe attack in the history of the Church.

It is marvelous to know that the Bible is gloriously withstanding this latest attempt to destroy it, as it has withstood all other attempts on the part of its enemies in the past.

The amazing scientific facts in the very structure of the Bible itself were no doubt intended to be revealed as a surprise weapon of combat for the final crisis. The Holy Spirit, Who caused these numerical features to be so arranged in the under structure of the Bible, evidently foresaw that there would come a day when destructive critics and modernists would tamper with His book, and would attempt to discredit it. He no doubt foresaw that there would come a day when organized Atheism and other "isms" would do their utmost to overthrow the Bible. Therefore He placed these series of divine marks in the very structure of the text to provide indisputable proof of its divine origin, and to insure its purity. He hid them in a mysterious way, and caused them to remain concealed until a set time—this particular time in the history of the Church when among many, respect for the Bible is gone— the very time when such evidence is most needed.

Modernists and higher critics began their destruc- tive work many years ago. However, it has been only during the past fifty years that their work has progressed rapidly and has been seriously felt. Is it not strange that at that very time—50 years ago— the divine numeric structure of the Bible was discov- ered? Is it not strange that the Science of Bible Numerics appears in an age of Science?

Is it not strange that at the very time when or- ganized Atheism was first making its plans to overthrow and control Russia, God was preparing a **Russian** to discover thousands of numerical facts—facts which would scientifically prove the supernatural origin and character of the Bible—facts which would shatter all the arguments of Atheists, Modernists and Higher Critics? Perhaps no country has been so anti-God, anti-Christian, and anti-Bible as modern day Russia. Is it not remarkable to think that God saw fit to send a man out of that very country, and convert him, and equip him with the ability to discover the divine numerical structure of the Bible? Certainly these newly discovered irrefutable facts are God's answer to Atheism, Higher Criticism, and Modernism.

Indeed, "God moves in mysterious ways His won ders to perform."

TWO THINGS FOR EVERY READER TO REMEMBER

(1) The scientific demonstration is convincing to all those who are willing to see.

(2) The demonstration will be opposed by some —by those who deliberately refuse to see.

(1) Mr. Panin's extraordinary Bible proof is not based on mere theories and convincing phrase- ology, but upon positive facts—facts which are present- ed according to the inexorable laws of logic. If a person will but open his eyes and acquaint himself with the facts—if he is willing to listen to reason—he is simply compelled to admit that Mr. Panin's facts prove that the Bible is not a human book, but a supernatural God breathed book. Mr. Panin presents an amazing proof—an actual demonstration according to the law of design, so simple that any school boy can easily understand it. The supernatural origin and character of the Bible are now convincingly and scientifically demonstrated to the complete satisfaction of any un- biased, open minded person.

(2) However, the fact that such an amazing scien- tific proof is available does not necessarily mean that all the atheists and infidels and higher critics of the world will now accept the Bible as a God given book—verbally inspired or breathed of God.

"The god of this world (Satan) hath blinded the minds of them that believe not, lest the light of the glorious gospel of Christ, who is the image of God, should shine unto them."—II Cor. 4:4.

"The natural man receiveth not the things of the Spirit of God: for they are foolishness unto him; neither can he know them, because they are spiritually discerned."—I Cor. 2:14.

"This is the condemnation, that light is come into the world, and men love darkness rather than light, because their deeds are evil."—John 3:19.

Readers should not be unduly alarmed or surprised when they find some who oppose this scientific demonstration. The Bible does not teach that all will accept the Scriptures and that all will be saved. The actual demonstration is convincing to every candid, open minded person—to everyone who is willing to "see" and believe. However, there are always some who deliberately refuse to see and believe regardless of how much convincing evidence is presented. Mr. Panin has given the facts to unbelievers, but the eyes for seeing them, only God can give. The scientific demonstration can never convince those who deliberately close their eyes to the truth and simply refuse to look. The fact that some do not want to be convinced is no argument against this amazing proof, for the irrefutable facts remain unaltered in the structure of the Scripture regardless of the opinion or attitude of unbelievers. Those who accept this demonstration are utterly helpless when they come to those who are not willing to listen. Persons who deliberately ignore the facts are in a pitiful state of affairs. Reason and logic mean nothing to them—they commit "intellectual suicide."

Readers should not be surprised or alarmed to find the amazing scientific demonstration subject to criticism and attack. Disbelievers in this proof of divine inspiration may not be satisfied with merely refusing to see for themselves, but, they may even go so far as to attempt to influence others against it. The proof is supremely important—and is bold and positive—it has vital bearing and effect upon every human being. Naturally open opposition to such proof can be expected. It must be remembered that it is Satan's business to foster doubt and unbelief. He has been busy causing mankind to question God's word since the beginning when he said, "Yea, hath God said?" Genesis 3:1. Satan always has fought and opposed every truth, every plan, and every action of God. We must be prepared to recognize the devil's work when it appears, and then say "Amen" to God's true Word. "All Scripture is given by inspiration of God."—II Timothy 3:16. "Yea, let God be true, but every man a liar."—Romans 3:4.

If the Bible itself is hated, misquoted, misrepresented, falsely accused, criticized and attacked, is it surprising that any proof of the Bible should escape false accusation and criticism? Throughout the centuries the Bible has been misrepresented and falsely accused, yet this has not affected the character of the Bible itself. The Scripture stands as pure and as spot-

less as ever. No one has discovered a single contradiction in it, or established a case against it. However,
the false accusations have deceived some, and have
caused some to reject the Bible. Any proof of the
Bible is subject to the same misrepresentation and false
accusation. The proof itself remains untouched, its
truth remains unaltered. However the false accusations
may deceive some, and may cause some to reject the
proof.

Those who disbelieve this demonstration may
openly "call" it a fraud, a lie, or a fake. It must be
remembered, however, that these words have never
yet established a single fact. Such words are not mentioned in books on logic as powerful and convincing
"methods" of demonstration and proof. Masters of
thought throughout the ages have considered such
terms as non-essentials in logical argument. Merely
"calling" something a fake or a fraud proves nothing.
Likewise, mere opinions or theories of men expressed
in apparently convincing phraseology prove nothing
Opinions are opinions and facts are facts. If the so-
called facts are **not** facts they can be disproved without difficulty. If they **are** facts we must answer to
God for ignoring them.

Some critics may propound and rely on "irrelevant" answers—answers which appear to have a vital
bearing on the subject, but in reality are only beside
the point. Such a "non-sequitur" is not sufficient to prove
anything. Persons may originate irrelevant answers
through their own misunderstanding, unfamiliarity or
ignorance of the subject. One can easily blunder by
basing his arguments on false premises.

If one were to find a few features of sevens scattered here and there in the text of some writing
outside the Bible, this would not be sufficient to disprove the scientific demonstration of the Bible. A
feature may occur accidentally here and there in some
other writing but the phenomena of the hundreds of
features in a single Bible text, and the phenomena of
the seemingly endless chains of intricate features which
run through all of the sixty-six Bible books (like that
of the word "Moses" for example, Chapter 4), could
never be reproduced in any human writing. The
phenomena of the order numbers of the words, and
the phenomena of the cross-section-check on the vocabulary and the hundreds of other systems of features
which intertwine all of the sixty-six books could never
be reproduced in any human writing.

Any who might feel inclined to criticize or condemn Mr. Panin's results should realize that his work was
not hurriedly or lightly done in a few months' time,
but was accomplished in a period which extended over
50 years. He is an expert and is the pioneer in his
particular field of work. He is acquainted with the
voluminous facts of his discoveries as no other person
is. Therefore a thoughtful person will "think twice"
and will carefully consider the matter before he seeks
to hastily criticize or to quickly pass judgment upon
the result of the 50 years' diligent, painstaking labor of
an expert.

What man, after spending merely days or weeks
or months of investigation, is capable of criticizing Mr.
Panin's fifty years' labor? If great scholars have not

attempted to disprove Mr. Panin's accuracy, should anyone with lack of evidence feel justified in attempting to condemn his lifetime discoveries?

ACKNOWLEDGMENT TO DR. IVAN PANIN

The writer acknowledges his great indebtedness to Mr. Panin who has made this book possible by so kindly giving him permission to use this numeric material. Mr. Panin has extended every courtesy and has most graciously given the writer access to all of his valuable manuscripts and numeric data. This permission is indeed deeply appreciated. For two and one-half years the writer has made a general study of Mr. Panin's work and has personally examined and studied many of the 40,000 pages of numeric data. However, as yet, he has only scratched the surface of the phenomenal numeric facts which Mr. Panin has unearthed.

The writer considers it a great privilege to have been permitted to confer personally with Dr. Panin. The personal acquaintance and instruction of this man of God have been a blessing which the writer can never forget or fully express in words..

Mr. Panin has not withheld his discoveries but has permitted them to be freely used by all Christians everywhere provided they are used for the glory of God. His work has been for the entire Church of Christ—for God's people everywhere. Therefore Mr. Panin has been strictly undenominational and non-sectarian. He is definitely a fundamental orthodox

Christian. However, he has never allowed himself or his work to be associated with any particular one of the many orthodox denominations. He has lectured freely among many of these fundamental religious `organizations but has kept himself and his work free from all denominational barriers and divisions of Christianity. In accordance with Mr. Panin's policy and wishes this book which contains his numeric discoveries is presented to the public without any denominational attachment.

DR. IVAN PANIN
Discoverer of the
Numerical Structure of the Bible

OTHER EVIDENCES OF DIVINE
INSPIRATION

The Bible differs from all other religious books in that it is supported by well grounded evidence. Some readers may not be aware of the fact that, in addition to the newly discovered scientific proof discussed in this book, there are numerous other evidences and proofs that the Bible is actually a supernatural, God inspired, God given book. Throughout the years there has accumulated an abundance of splendid evidence. Some of these other proofs are: fulfilled prophecy, the scientific accuracy of the Bible, its historical accuracy as revealed by archæology, the marvelous unity of the Bible, its inexhaustible depths, its indestructibility, its superior teaching, its matchless influence, the absence of a single contradiction, the testimony of Christ, the character of Christ, the testimony of vital personal experience, etc.

A comprehensive and detailed presentation of any one of these subjects requires a great deal of space—in fact, volumes have been devoted to some of these interesting and convincing Bible proofs. They have been mentioned here merely because some readers may have been hitherto uninformed of their existence, and may be interested in study along those lines.

THE BIBLE

"Bad men or devils would not have written the Bible for it condemns them and their work.

"Good men or angels could not have written it, for in saying that it was from God when it was their own invention, they would have been guilty of falsehood and could not have been good.

"The only remaining Being Who could have written it is GOD!"

—FLAVEL

CHAPTER NINE

How Do The Newly Discovered Facts Affect Us?

We have seen before our very eyes an actual scientific demonstration of the divine verbal inspiration of the Bible—a demonstration consisting of facts discovered beneath the very surface of the original Bible text. We have learned that these amazing facts demonstrate that even every "jot" and "tittle" (the smallest letter and the smallest mark) of the Bible is inspired of God.

Dear reader, these newly discovered facts have a vital relationship to every human being. They affect each and every one of us in a very definite way. Why? Because in proving the great truth of the divine inspiration of the Bible they place upon each of us a certain responsibility—a responsibility which cannot be avoided.

If we gain knowledge that the Bible is a supernatural, God inspired book—the very Word of God Himself—a strange thing happens. Knowledge of this great truth never leaves us where it finds us—we never remain as we were before. Such knowledge **bestows a privilege, it opens an opportunity, it creates a responsibility to examine and heed the instructions God has given us in His Word.**

Once we know that the Bible is God's Word the issue can never end at that point. Merely acknowledging that the Bible is divine is not sufficient. If we are to be consistent and honest with ourselves we must continue one step farther—we must learn and accept what God has to say concerning us in His Word. If the Bible were a mere human production we would be under no obligation to give any special attention to it. However, inasmuch as it is divine we cannot justly disregard its contents and we cannot casually lay it aside saying that it has no special relationship to us.

It is our duty to know, believe, and obey the instructions God has given in His Word.

The Bible gives God's message to all humanity. It tells us the purpose for which the Scriptures were written. It tells us why some cannot understand the Bible. It tells why some do not think as the Bible teaches. It tells why some dislike the Bible and why some condemn its teaching. Most important of all is the fact that it gives a perfect picture and description of ourselves—it enables us to see ourselves as we really are and it enables us to know of our future.

When the Bible makes a statement, every word of that statement can be relied upon as true. Being of divine origin, it speaks with sovereign authority. It speaks without apology. The teachings of the Bible are not complicated and difficult to understand, for the Author of the Book, the Holy Spirit of God, promises that all who humbly come to its pages will be guided and enlightened in understanding its teachings.

There are various Bible statements which vitally concern our eternal well-being. Let us examine these statements in a spirit of honesty and truth.

Many have asked the question—

Why Was The Bible Written?

God clearly states His purpose in giving the Bible to mankind.

"Written that ye might believe that Jesus is the Christ, the Son of God; and that believing **ye might have life** through his name." John 20:31

From this verse of Scripture we learn that "life" is obtained through believing in Jesus Christ.

"that believing (in Jesus Christ) ye might have **life** through his name."

We shall learn that the "life" mentioned in this passage is not "physical life," but "spiritual life." The fact that we have physical life does not necessarily mean that we also have spiritual life for the Scripture bears out the strange truth that individuals may be alive physically and yet be "dead" spiritually.

"**dead** in your sins"—Col. 2:13
"**dead** in trespasses and sins"—Eph. 2:1
"**dead** in sins,"—Eph. 2:5
"**dead** while she liveth"—1 Tim. 5:6

By nature we are "dead" spiritually.

"Wherefore, as by one man sin entered into the world, and **death** by sin; and so death passed upon **all men**"—Rom. 5:12; II Cor. 5:14

By nature we are "sinners."

"**all** have sinned"—Rom. 5:12
"**all** (are) under sin"—Rom. 3:9
"**all** have sinned and come short of the glory of God."—Rom. 3:23
"the scripture hath concluded **all** under sin"—Gal. 3:22
"there is no man that sinneth not"—I Kings 8:46
"there is not a just man upon the earth, that doeth good, and sinneth not."—Ecc. 7:20
"There is none righteous, no, not one."—Rom. 3:10
"If we say we have no sin we deceive ourselves."—I John 1:8
"If we say we have not sinned, we make him (Christ) a liar."—I John 1:10

Sin is a sad and terrible reality.   This fact is proved not only by the teaching of Scripture but also by the testimony of all mankind.   All have been hounded by remorse of conscience for wrong-doing.

By nature we are "lost"

We are "**guilty before God**."—Rom. 3:19
We are "**condemned already**."—John 3:18
As sinnners we are "**unjust**" in God's sight.
  I Peter 3:18
  ("There is **not a just** man upon the earth"—

Ecc. 7:20. "There is **none righteous**, no not one."—Rom. 3:10)

Our hearts are **"not right in the sight of God."**—Acts 8:21; Ps. 78:37

Our hearts are "deceitful . . . and **desperately wicked"**—Mt. 15:19

By nature we are **"sold under sin"**—Rom. 7:14; Is. 52:3

We are the **"servants of sin"**—Rom. 6:17; Jn. 8:34

We are "holden (bound or held captive) by the **cords of sin."**—Prov. 5:22

As sinners we are abiding in **"darkness"**—I Pet. 2:9; Eph. 5:8

Sins **"have separated"** us from God. There is no communion or fellowship with Him.—Is. 59:2

By nature we are **"far off"** from God—Eph. 2:13 and are **"lost"**—Lu. 19:10

We are **"without Christ, . . . having no hope."**

We are **"without God** in the world."—Eph. 2:12

By nature we are helpless and hopeless sinners. We are dead spiritually and are guilty and unjust before God. We are separated or alienated from God and have no communion or fellowship with Him. We are lost "having no hope."

It is a precious truth to know that irrespective of our state and condition by nature—

God loves us.

"God commendeth **his love toward us,** . . . while we were yet sinners."—Rom. 5:8

"Herein is love, not that we loved God, but that **He loved us."**—I John 4:10

"In this was manifest **the love of God toward us,** because that God sent His only begotten Son into the world that we might live through him." —I John 4:9

"For God so loved the world, that he gave his only begotten Son, that whosoever believeth in him should not perish, but have everlasting life."—John 3:16

"Behold, what **manner of love** the Father hath bestowed **upon us,** that we should be called the sons of God."—I John 3:1

For What Purpose Did The Son Of God Come To This Earth?

Christ came to accomplish a definite work. He came to provide "salvation" for sinners.

"Jesus Christ came into the world to **save sinners."** I Tim. 1:15

Christ "is come to **seek and to save** that which is **lost."**—Lu. 19:10; Mt. 11:18

"God sent . . . his Son into the world . . . that the world through him might be **saved."** Jn. 3:17; Jn. 12:47

"The Father sent the Son to be the **Saviour** of the world."—I Jn. 4:14

Christ came "to make **reconciliation for the sins** of the people."—Heb. 2:17

"God . . . sent his Son to be the **propitiation** for **our sins."**—I Jn. 4:10

"He was manifested **to take away our sins."** —I Jn. 3:5

"I am come that they might have **life.**"—Jn. 10:10
"God sent his only begotten Son into the world
that we might **live** through him."—I Jn. 4:9

By Coming To This Earth How Did Christ Make It Possible For Sinners To Be "Saved?"

How did He accomplish the work which He came
to do?

The Son of God did **not** accomplish this great
work by coming to this earth to be a **"good example"**
or a **"great religious teacher."** Neither did He accomplish this work by giving the world **"noble phil-
osophical principles."** There is a far deeper meaning
involved than this.

Christ, the sinless Son of God, as "a lamb
without spot or blemish" gave Himself on the cross
as a sacrifice for sin. He, the innocent party, became
the sin bearer for the guilty.

(I) By His Death on the Cross
Christ became our Saviour

"His own self **bare our sins in his own body** on
the tree (cross)"—I Peter 2:24
"He (God) hath made Him (Christ) **to be sin
for us.**"—I Cor. 5:21
"The Lord (God) hath **laid on Him (Christ) the
iniquity of us all.**"—Is 53:6
"Christ **died for the ungodly.**"—Rom. 5:6
"While we were yet **sinners** Christ **died for us.**"
Rom. 5:8
"Christ hath once suffered for sins, the **just**

(Christuit) for the unjust (sinners)"—I Pet. 3:18
Also Tit. 2:14, Gal. 1:4, I Cor. 15:3, I Cor. 5:21,
I John 3:16

(II) By His Death on the Cross
Christ Shed His Blood For Us

(a) Through the shed blood of Christ
   —We are "redeemed"

"Thou (Christ) was slain and thou hast redeemed
us to God by thy **blood**."—Rev. 5:9
"We have **redemption** through His **blood**."—Col.
1:14; Eph. 1:7
"Ye were not **redeemed** with corruptible things
such as **silver or gold,** but (ye were redeemed)
with the **precious blood of Christ** as of a lamb
without spot and without blemish.'—I Pet. 1:13
"Ye have sold yourselves for nought and ye shall
be **redeemed** without money."—Is. 52:3
"By His own **blood** He . . . obtained eternal
redemption for us."—Heb. 9:11

Notice the following important truth in regard to
"redemption."

"Ye are not your own, For ye are **bought** with
a **price**."—I Cor. 6:19-20
The Church of God Christ "hath **purchased** with
His own **blood**."—Acts 20:28
Christ "gave His life a **ransom**"—Mt. 20:28
He "gave Himself a **ransom**"—I Tit. 2:6

These Scripture references using the words
redeemed, ransomed, bought, purchased, are particularly significant.

Redeemed means bought back. Sinners are sold under sin (Rom. 6:17 - Isa. 52:3) but are redeemed by Christ's blood. Sinners could be redeemed or purchased from their guilty, sinful, lost and condemned condition, only by some Person paying the **price.** Christ paid the price to redeem sinners. The price which He paid was not silver or gold (I Pet. 1:13) or money (Isa. 52:3) but was His own **shed blood**—His own **life.**

(b) Through the shed blood of Christ
—**We have the "forgiveness" or "remission" of our sins**

"**My blood** of the new testament (covenant) **is shed** for many **for the remission of sins.**"
—Mt. 26:28
"In whom we have redemption **through His (Christ's) blood,** the forgiveness of sins."
—Eph. 1:7; Col. 1:14

(c) Through the shed blood of Christ
—**We are cleansed from sin**

"Jesus Christ . . . loved us, and **washed us** from our sins in His own **blood.**"—Rev. 1:5
"The **blood** of Jesus Christ His (God's) Son cleanseth us from **all sin.**"—II Jn. 1:7

(d) Through the shed blood of Christ
—**We are "justified" (made "just") before God and are "reconciled" to God.**
"Being now **justified** by His **blood.**"—Rom. 5:9
"When we were yet enemies, we were **reconciled to God** by the **death of His Son.**"—Rom. 5:10

(e) Through the shed blood of Christ
—We are made "nigh" to God

> "But now in Christ Jesus ye who sometimes were far off are **made nigh (brought close to God) by the blood** of Christ."—Eph. 2:13

(f) Through the shed blood of Christ
—We make peace with God

> "**Having made peace** through the **blood** of His Cross." —Col. 1:20

We have seen what **Christ has done** to provide for our salvation, now—

What must we do to be saved?

The Bible teaches that this salvation cannot be earned or merited by good works or deeds.

> "**Not by works of righteousness which we have done,** but according to His mercy He saved us." —Titus 3:5
>
> "saved . . . **not of works,** lest any man should boast."—Eph. 2:8
>
> "Who hath saved us . . . **not according to works.**" II Tim. 1:8
>
> Our good works or our righteousness will not obtain salvation for us, for our "righteousness is as filthy rags in His sight."—Isa. 64:6

Salvation is the "gift of God" therefore it cannot be earned or merited. If we could earn our own salvation it would not have been necessary for Christ to have died.

Alas, how many depend upon their own self-righteousness for salvation. Many depend upon their church membership. Others depend upon their good living—in being respectable citizens of the community—in supporting their families, and in contributing to the poor and to the up-keep of the church.

A way of salvation which a person devises for himself, even though there is much good about it, will never bring the soul to God.

Man's way of salvation by "works" is not God's way.

> "There is a way that seemeth right unto a man, but the end thereof are the ways of death."
> —Prov. 14:12

> "My thoughts are not your thoughts, neither are your ways my ways, saith the Lord. For as the heavens are higher than the earth, so are my ways higher than your ways, and my thoughts than your thoughts."—Isa. 55:8-9

We Are Saved By Faith—By Believing In Christ's Finished Work of Redemption, And By Receiving Him As Our Personal Saviour

(a) **We must believe in the work of Christ.**

> "**Believe** on the Lord Jesus Christ, and thou shalt be **saved**."—Acts 16:31
> "Through his name whosoever **believeth in him** shall receive **the remission of sins**."
> "And **by him** all that **believeth** are **justified** from all things."—Acts 13:36
> "Without faith it is impossible to please God."

Genuine faith in the work of Christ will be accom-
panied by repentance.

"God commandeth all men everywhere to repent."
—Acts 17:30

"Godly sorrow worketh repentance to salvation."
—II Cor. 7:9-10

The words of the publican express the thought.
"God be merciful to me a sinner."—Lu. 18:13

"If we confess our sins, he is faithful and just to
forgive us our sins, and to cleanse us from all
unrighteousness."—I Jn. 1:9

"Repent . . . for the remission of sins."—Acts 2:38

"Repent . . . that your sins may be blotted out."
—Acts 3:19

"Except ye repent ye shall all likewise perish."
—Lu. 13:3

(b) We must receive Christ as our personal Saviour.

By nature we are "dead" spiritually. To become
alive spiritually we must be born of God. We must
be "born again." As we can enter this world only by
the process of a natural birth, so we can enter the
Kingdom of God only by the process of a spiritual
birth. Spiritual life is received only by the spiritual
birth.

"That which is born of the flesh is flesh and that
which is born of the Spirit is spirit."—John 3:6. To
be saved—to be a child of God—we must be "born
of God."—John 1:13

Christ said, "Verily, verily I say unto thee except
a man be born again he cannot see the kingdom of God."—John3 :3

Regeneration or the "new birth" is not baptism, or confirmation, neither is it reformation.
Regeneration is not the old nature altered, reformed
or re-invigorated. It is not a reforming process on the
part of man, and it is not a natural foreward step in
man's development. Regeneration is a new birth from
above, and is a supernatural creative act on the part
of God. The sinner receives a new nature—God's
nature, and he is a new creature, and puts on the
new man which God creates after holiness and righteousness.

"A new heart will I give you, and a new spirit
will I put within you;" Eze. 36:26. "If any man be
in Christ, he is a new creature; old things pass away
and behold all things become new." II Cor. 5:17.
Eph. 4:24.

By regeneration, or new birth, we are admitted
into the kingdom of God. There is no other way of
becoming a Christian but by being born from above.
Too often we find other things, such as good works,
reformation or baptism, substituted by man for God's
appointed way of becoming a child of God. To be
a child of God one must be born of the Spirit of God.

Jesus said, "Except a man be born again he cannot see the kingdom of God." No age, sex, position,
condition, exempts anyone from this necessity. Not
to be born again is to be lost. There is no substitute
for the new birth. Paul said, "Neither circumcision
availeth anything nor uncircumcision, **but a new creature.**" That is the all important thing, being a new
creature in Christ. Christ did not say that ye ought

to be born again, or it would be good for you to be born again. He said "ye must be born again." Jn. 3:7.

We can experience this new birth by receiving Christ as our personal Saviour.

John 1:12 tells us, "As many as received Him (Christ) to them gave He power to become the sons (children) of God, even to them that believe on his name."

We cannot receive eternal life without receiving Christ. "God hath given to us eternal life, and this life is in His Son, He that hath the Son hath life, and he that hath not the Son of God hath not life." I John 5:11-12.

"Verily, verily, I say unto you, He that believeth on me hath everlasting life."—Jn. 6:47

We will experience this new birth—we will be born of God—if we receive Christ as our Saviour. We will be new creatures in Christ Jesus, "and old things will pass away and behold all things will become new." II Cor. 5:17. Christ will dwell in us. Gal. 2:20. And we "shall not come into condemnation (judgment) but are passed from death unto life." Jn. 5:24.

One of the most wonderful facts about this salvation is that it is for everyone. "God is no respecter of persons." Acts 10:34. "Whosoever shall call upon the name of the Lord shall be saved." Acts 2:21. Christ encouragingly calls, "Come unto me all ye that labor and are heavy laden and I will give you rest." Mt. 11:28. "Him that cometh unto me I will in no wise cast out." Jn. 6:37. Rev. 3:20; 22:17.

We can know that we are saved, and we can know Christ as our personal Saviour. I Jn. 5:10, "He that believeth on the Son of God hath the witness within himself." Rom. 7:1-16, "The Spirit itself beareth witness with our spirit that we are the children of God."

Dear reader, there is no middle territory, you are either saved or you are not saved. The Bible says, "No servant can serve two masters; . . . ye cannot serve God and mammon." Lu. 16:13. Christ said, "He that is not with me is against me." Lu. 11:23. "Know ye not, that to whom ye yield yourselves servants to obey, his servants ye are to whom ye obey: whether of sin unto death, or of obedience unto righteousness?" Rom. 6:16.

The Bible also says, "Choose ye this day whom ye shall serve." Joshua 24:15. "Now is the accepted time, now is the day of salvation." "Today if ye hear His voice, harden not your hearts." Heb. 3:7. Do not postpone accepting Christ. "Seek ye the Lord while He may be found, call upon Him while He is near." Isa. 55:6. "Ye know not what shall be on the morrow. Jas. 4:14.

"For what shall it profit a man, if he shall gain the whole world, and lose his own soul? Or what shall a man give in exchange for his soul?"

"Come now, and let us reason together, saith the Lord: though your sins be as scarlet, they shall be as white as snow; though they be red like crimson, they shall be as wool." Isa. 1:18. "This is a faithful say-ing, and worthy of all acceptation, that Christ Jesus came into the world to save sinners; of whom I am chief." 1 Tim. 1:15.

Why are Men Lost?

"Because they believe not on Me" John 16:9. "He that believeth not the Son shall not see life: but the wrath of God abideth on him." John 3:36

ADDENDA

Examples of Facts Discovered Beneath the Surface of the Book of Mark

The following are abbreviated examples of the same type of numerical discoveries as are presented in Chapter Three—discoveries of numerical facts which are hidden in the very structure of **single Bible passages.**

BOOK OF MARK, CHAPTER ONE, VERSES 1-8

FEATURE ONE
The total number of Greek words in these first eight verses is exactly ....126 or 18 7's

FEATURE TWO
The number of Greek letters in these 126 words is ....427 or 61 7's

FEATURE THREE
The number of vowels in these 427 letters is ....224 or 32 7's
The number of consonants in these 427 letters is ....203 or 29 7's

FEATURE FOUR

The number of syllables in
the 126 Greek words of the
passage is exactly 294   or   42   7's

FEATURE FIVE

Of the 126 words in the passage, the number which begin
with a vowel is exactly 42   or   6   7's
Of these 126 words, the
number which begin with a
consonant is 84   or   12   7's

FEATURE SIX

The number of vocabulary
words in the passage is exactly.........77   or   11   7's

FEATURE SEVEN

Of these 77 Greek vocabu-
lary words, the number John
used in his speech is exactly 21   or   3   7's

FEATURE EIGHT

Of these 77 vocabulary words
found in the first eight verses
of Mark, the number in
verses 1-5 (a natural divi-
sion) is exactly 49   or   7   7's
The number of vocabulary
words in verses 6-8 (also a
natural division) is 28   or   4   7's

FEATURE NINE
Of the 77 Greek vocabulary
words, the number which be-
gin with a vowel is exactly............42   or   6   7's
The number of words which
begin with a consonant is 35   or   5   7's

FEATURE TEN
The number of Greek letters
in the longest word in this
passage is 14   or   2   7's

It is needless to weary the reader with further
enumeration of the numeric features which occur beneath the surface of these first eight verses in Mark.
Nearly all given so far are features of the vocabulary
alone.   The next natural paragraph following these
first eight verses consists of verses 9, 10, 11.   A few
examples are given from this paragraph.

BOOK OF MARK, CHAPTER ONE
VERSES 9, 10, 11

The Baptism of Christ

FEATURE ONE
The number of Greek vocab-
ulary words in this passage is........35   or   5   7's

FEATURE TWO
The numeric value of the
passage is exactly 27,783   or   3,969   7's

FEATURE THREE
The numeric value of the
forms in which these 35
words are found is exactly ......26,887 or 3,841   7's

MARK, CHAPTER TWO, VERSES 13-20

Following are a few examples of the many numerical features which occur beneath the surface of these five verses.

FEATURE ONE
The number of Greek vocabulary words in these five
verses is exactly ....49 or   7   7's

FEATURE TWO
Of the 49 vocabulary words
the number used by Christ
is exactly ....14 or   2   7's

FEATURE THREE
The number of words used
by the Scribes is exactly...................7

MARK, CHAPTER THREE, VERSES 13-19

This passage gives the account of Christ appointing the twelve apostles. Their names are Simon, James, John, Andrew, Philip, Bartholomew, Matthew, Thomas, James, Thaddeus, Simon, and Judas. It is amazing to note that:

The numeric value of these twelve Greek names is a number which divides per- fectly by seven. Their nu- meric value is exactly ....9,639 or 1,377   7's

This is only one of the many numeric features which have been discovered in these twelve names. Only one example is given from each of the following two passages.

MARK, CHAPTER FOUR, VERSES 3-20

In these verses Christ relates the parable of the sower.

The number of Greek vocab- ulary words in the parable is exactly ....49 or   7   7's

MARK, CHAPTER THIRTEEN, VERSES 5-37

These verses contain the speech of Christ.

The number of Greek vocab- ulary words in this passage is exactly ....203 or   29   7's

NOTES

NOTES